C000017375

This book does a great job of bringing togeth[...]
mindfulness and Otto Scharmer's powerful [...]
managers in coping with the increasing stre[...]
Edgar H. Schein, Professor Emeritus, MIT Sloan School of Management. Author
of "Organizational Culture and Leadership" and of "Humble Inquiry: The Gentle
Art of Asking instead of Telling."

Just imagine if a good proportion of leaders in all sectors really were mindful –
self-aware, resilient, open and less imprisoned either by habits or hang-ups?
How different would the world be? Wibo Koole's book rightly asks us to see
this as an achievable goal, and provides pointers as to how it could be achieved.
Geoff Mulgan, Chief Executive of Nesta, and author of "The Locust and the Bee."

Filled with practical insights and a wealth of practical tools based on his
experiences as a company director and mindfulness teacher, Wibo Koole
shows us how mindfulness enables leaders and their organizations to tackle
and become freed from deep-rooted, limiting patterns of behavior. A
compelling and inspirational read for leaders of all kinds.
Lisa Lahey is a faculty member at the Harvard Graduate School of Education,
co-founder of MINDS AT WORK®, and author (with Robert Kegan) of
"Immunity to Change," and other books that help people to close the gap between
their good intentions and behavior.

"Mindful Leadership" points at the biggest leverage point we have for initiating
and sustaining positive change: our awareness. This much-needed book
provides insights, tools and practices for how to create awareness as leaders and
teams in organizations, and shows how mindful leaders can foster a culture of
awareness-based strategy development in organizations.
Otto Scharmer, senior lecturer at the Massachusetts Institute of Technology and
author of "Theory U, Learning from the Future as It Emerges," of "Leading from
the Emerging Future. From ego-system to eco-system economy" (with Katrin
Kaufer), and of "Presence" (with Peter Senge, Betty Sue Flowers, and Joseph
Jaworksi).

In our rapidly changing world, leadership requires that our minds be flexible
and open like never before. But how? Mindfulness training helps us meet the
inevitable challenges of our lives with curiosity, ease, courage, and warmth.
Wibo Koole expertly guides the reader into core concepts and practices that
have the power to transform individuals and their teams, both inside and out.
Christopher Germer, PhD, clinical instructor, Harvard Medical School, author of
"The Mindful Path to Self-Compassion," and co-editor of "Mindfulness and
Psychotherapy."

In an age where we are constantly confronted with even bigger and more complex interconnected challenges, true leadership makes the difference. Leadership that is on a constant mindful journey to see the whole and the parts, to explore and know yourself while recognizing and connecting with others. Wibo gives in his book a very compelling and practical description of how leaders can shift their mindset and become more resilient, have unconditional responsibility, and become more innovative and connecting. It starts with yourself, and it is the most rewarding journey of all.

Lucas Simons, founder and CEO of NewForesight and SCOPEinsight, Young Global Leader – World Economic Forum (2011), Ashoka Fellow, and former director UTZ Certified.

Bringing the wisdom of mindfulness meditation to the challenges of leading organizations has finally found traction in business schools, law firms, hospitals, board rooms, and more and Wibo's contribution to this trend is central. I highly recommend exploring the topic of mindful leadership and this book is an excellent guide.

Michael Carroll, author of "The Mindful Leader."

What were once esoteric teachings of Buddhism are now commonplace in school, hospitals, and boardrooms. In a clear and concise way, Wibo Koole demystifies mindfulness and explains how it can make a measurable difference in organizational leadership.

Jay Michaelson, author of "Evolving Dharma: Meditation, Buddhism and the Next Generation of Enlightenment."

While many managers have intelligence, experience, and interpersonal skills, truly outstanding leaders possess something rarer and more important: deep wisdom. In this clear, practical, step-by-step guide, Wibo Koole shows us how to use the power of mindfulness to develop managerial wisdom – the ability to see the big picture and respond skillfully to challenges rather than react out of our fear or egoistic concerns. It's a must-read for anyone who wants to be a wiser, happier, and more effective leader.

Ronald D. Siegel, Psy. D. assistant clinical professor of psychology, Harvard Medical School, and author of "The Mindfulness Solution: Everyday Practices for Everyday Problems."

Wibo has written a book that is practical, grounded and urgently needed. In mindful leadership lies the answer to many of humanity's challenges, making this a much-needed book.

Zaid Hassan, co-founder and partner of Reos consultants, and author of "The Social Labs Revolution."

Mindful Leadership

Effective tools to help you focus and succeed

Wibo Koole

Warden Press

© 2014 Wibo Koole, Amsterdam, the Netherlands
ISBN: 978-94-92004-00-0
Original title: *Mindful leiderschap. Voor effectieve teams en organisaties.*
Business Contact, Amsterdam, 2013
This edition published by Warden Press / Wardy Poelstra, Amsterdam
Translated from the Dutch by Jonathan Ellis, Wierden
Cover design: Pankra / Robert Jan van Noort, The Hague
Photo author: Jessica Hooghiemstra, Amsterdam
Interior design / lay-out: Elgraphic bv, Vlaardingen

All rights reserved. No part of this publication may be reproduced,
stored in a retrieval system, or transmitted in any form or by any
means, electronic, mechanical, photocopying, recording or otherwise
without the prior written permission of the publisher.

Table of Contents

Chapter 4. Mindfully Managing Teams

Chapter 5. Charting a Course with Full Attention

Epilogue: Mastering Mindful Leadership

Introduction

"It's just paying attention, on purpose, in the present moment, and non-judgmentally to the unfolding of experience moment to moment."[1]

Jon Kabat-Zinn, founder of mindfulness training.

My body felt heavy and incapable of much action. And that at the very moment, in the summer of 2005, when I was about to embark on a new, exciting adventure: setting up my own company, Create2connect. I had spent the past ten years working day and night as campaign and strategy manager for the Dutch Consumers' Association; but instead of feeling a rush of fresh, new energy, I just lay there on the sofa, debilitated, hardly able to pick up the books I had so looked forward to reading.

Apparently I was completely exhausted – both physically and mentally. And that rather surprised me: I'm a regular jogger and I'm in fairly good condition. What's more, I had participated in a number of management development programs and built up a fairly good insight into myself. But without seeing it coming, I had fallen into one of the most pervasive traps of leadership: sacrificing yourself out of a feeling of responsibility and accepting all the exhaustion that came with it.

I put it down to the constant changes in the organization. To new demands for information from our clients. The emergence

---

1   Jon Kabat-Zinn, "Mindfulness-based interventions in context: past, present, and future," *Clinical Psychology: Science and Practice* 10, no. 2 (2003): 145.

of new technology, having to work faster and more flexibly. They were challenging and exciting times, and I wanted to take full responsibility for things together with my team.

Fortunately, I quickly recuperated and got back into the swing of things. The question of how to prevent this surfaced again just over a year later when I began mindfulness training. I experienced how attention exercises were an important means of making timely adjustments to your stress housekeeping. But more than that, they sharpened my awareness of everything that was happening around me and therefore inside me.

I had the feeling that I had come across something that, despite all the leadership training programs I had followed, I had missed in my management role: a sensitive antenna for everything happening around me and how I was coping with it myself. I regularly reacted from what I thought something should be rather than from a clear experience of what was actually happening. And that meant that as a manager I had been functioning less effectively than I could have.

At the end of the training, I asked myself whether I could employ mindfulness in my work as interim manager and management consultant. And I found that I could. It allows you to lead intensive change processes with much more attention to what is really happening with people in the organization and to be more open to the demands made by your surroundings. With greater awareness and resilience. It is also something I recognize in people I have assisted as a consultant and who have followed a mindfulness training program.

Permanently subject to change

The constant change in the organization that I experienced as a manager at the Dutch Consumers' Association, is now found in all organizations. Change has become the status quo. It seems as if, in the day-to-day work of many organizations, not a single process can be carried out any longer according to strict rules; and policy changes are the order of the day. Innovation has become a must – whether to address the competitive struggle in the market or to adapt to new technologies. The result is that organizational structures are constantly changing. One month a team can be part of department X and the next it reports to department Y or has been integrated into a completely different structure. Making labor more flexible, supported by the possibilities of web-based work in the cloud, is the new way of organizing work, independent of time and place.

As all these changes take place, managers and teams are expected to deliver excellent operational performances with a high level of reliability. Technology and people must work perfectly together and failure is not tolerated, for it has enormous consequences. Just think of a disruption on the railroads or at a cell phone provider. Or even worse, in a surgical team at a hospital.

Teams must work more intensively and more intelligently together on their performance. Working on your own, individually at your own desk, is something that happens much less frequently; you are part of a team in a larger chain. Mutual relationships shift from hierarchical to horizontal and that means that, as manager, you share the managing and monitoring tasks with your team members. Collaborating and managing make a much greater demand on everybody's emotional intelligence to get things done.

Creativity and the ability to innovate must increase in response to rapid economic and social change. This is dictated by competition, by changes in policy instigated by political decisions or the media. An increasing number of products and services demand a smarter, more attractive and qualitatively better design if they are to satisfy the needs of the customer. In addition, organizations are expected to be fully aware of their relationship with the environment, to take into account issues regarding climate, water, biodiversity, raw materials and social diversity and equality in everything you do. Leadership must be constantly aware of what the organization is doing and which direction should be taken, ultimately under penalty of losing the *license to operate*.

In light of this need for permanent change, it is hardly surprising that pressure of work and stress remain high. 40% of Dutch employees and companies see work pressure as a major risk. Emotional strain, particularly in care and social services, is an additional factor. It leads to serious problems with health: in 2010, 43% of sickness absence days in the Netherlands were related to workload, work stress and physically demanding work.[2] Mental overload is also increasing. Although people generally feel healthy, they also admit that mentally their work is frequently extremely demanding. At the end of the day, they are worn out. Or, when they think of work, they simply can't face the start of a new day. The costs of absenteeism are high: employers could save up to one billion Euros a year.[3]

That organizations are permanently subject to change means that people in organizations must change with them. But that change process is not all that easy and that is the major challenge for leadership. To keep an eye on the surroundings and at the same time change.

Leadership: beyond the autopilot

Agreeable work with less stress, achieving higher reliability of operational processes, much more intensive teamwork with horizontal responsibilities, and a greater call for creativity and innovation. We also have high expectations of managers, for they can guide their teams and organizations in the proper direction, or they can slow them down in the delivery of performances and setting out innovative courses. Many actions are, therefore, undertaken to boost team performances, managers work on their competencies or change programs are implemented.

And yet, in our daily work, we see that it is far from easy to provide leadership for those changes. Again and again we see organizations and their leaders fall into the same old traps. Apparently, as manager, you are not sufficiently aware of the emotional reality of your team, and the result is a spate of trouble and inadequate performances. Or the top management of an organization does not succeed in keeping an open mind as it tries to focus on customers

2   TNO, *Arbobalans 2011* (2012). 19.
3   Ibid. 51-52.

and the social environment, resulting in the competition grabbing the lion's share of the market or government policy proving completely redundant.

At the heart of this is what I call the autopilot of routine, which encourages you to trust in what you already know rather than seeing the signals of the change that are on the horizon. Managers are so busy being busy that they forget to take time out for reflection. And often forget that when change happens they, as manager or leader, have to change along with everybody else.

Now, managers and leaders of organizations can handle a lot; they are very good at persevering. That's why they were chosen. But enduring stress and persevering under pressure is something other than coping with it smartly and effectively. And you need to free yourself more from your autopilot. You must be able to deal consciously and attentively with your role, know what you're doing, strengthen your physical and mental resilience, and be able to concentrate not only your attention but also the attention of your team or organization on the right things. And for that you need mindfulness. Mindfulness as the basis for leadership that shifts the attention towards unknown territory, without losing sight of the here and now. For in that unknown territory lie the solutions with which organizations can create value for their customers and their social environment.

Mindful leadership ensures that teams and organizations have a broad awareness of what they are doing. And for that they must learn to switch between action and reflection. Mindfulness enables that by strengthening physical and mental resilience, increasing the presence of mind to see what is really happening and taking responsibility for it. And this makes it possible for them to investigate what is necessary with an open mind and discover while innovating what works best.

What you train when you train mindfulness

Mindfulness enables you to escape your autopilot and consciously switch between action and reflection. In essence, mindfulness helps you learn how you can mentally switch your focus. You develop a greater awareness of your mind and, as a manager you can use this to direct your team or organization in a far better way.

In 2010, the British Mental Health Foundation published a review of scientific research into the effects of exercising mindfulness. Participants in such training at work reported 31% fewer medical symptoms, 17% reduction in "daily problems" and 31% fewer cases of a psychological nature. Three months later, the improvements were even more pronounced. Compared to the control group, participants in mindfulness training saw an increase in their ability to concentrate and had greater effectiveness of the immune system, for example against flu.[4] And so there is every reason to give mindfulness a place in the development of a culture in which work pressure, stress, and mental strain can be coped with more effectively.

Other research shows that exercising mindfulness leads to a greater processing capacity in the brain and therefore to higher quality decision-making. It sharpens your perception of matters that deviate from what you expect and helps you see that something must be done; not put things off, but signal and intervene. That is true in hospitals and on the deck of an aircraft carrier or for a large banking system, but equally for customer services at an internet provider, where you must be highly skilled in the interaction between technology and people in order to perform excellently.

Mindfulness also offers teams and their leaders the chance to deal more intelligently with each other, because it increases their emotional intelligence and their ability to work together in a smart and relaxed way. It is with good reason that Google has developed a program for emotional intelligence for its employees based on mindfulness, *Search Inside Yourself*. An extensive program of meditation and yoga offers Google employees the room to excel not only in software technology but also in social skills. With enormous success![5]

Mindfulness offers employees and leaders in organizations great-

4   Mental Health Foundation, *Be Mindful Report 2010* (2010). 30.
5   Chade-Meng Tan, *Search inside Yourself* (New York: HarperCollins, 2012).

er possibilities for breaking free of a rigid and closed mindset and creating an open, innovative mindset. Mindfulness breaks through existing patterns and gives people and organizations the possibility of responding consciously to the challenges from the environment. It creates an "open mind" for the future.

Jon Kabat-Zinn, founder of mindfulness training in its current form, describes mindfulness as *"paying attention in a special way: on purpose, in the present moment, and non-judgmentally."*[6] What is most striking in this description is its simplicity and directness. It is about an action done on purpose. Paying attention and observing what is happening to you, nothing more.

Being mindful actually means that you *don't* do certain things: you don't allow yourself to be swept along in mental diversions and express no judgment about what happens to you. Each thought, sensation, or each feeling that arises in your field of attention is recognized and accepted as it is.

This being observant, the state of mindfulness, also allows you to observe your feelings or thoughts as events in the mind, without strongly associating yourself with them and without reacting in a familiar automatic pattern. This calm way of reacting gives rise to a moment of pause between observation and response. And so mindfulness makes it possible for you to provide a more thoughtful answer to a situation instead of a reflex.[7] In short, you learn to concentrate on switching between action and reflection, between doing and being.

The advantages of this can be felt both on a personal level and on the level of team and organization. As examples, I'd like to give a number of reactions from people who attended our mindfulness training for managers:

"I notice that I am developing a different energy management system. Less stressed."
"I see that I react more consciously."

6 Jon Kabat-Zinn, *Waar je ook gaat, daar ben je* (Utrecht: Servire, 2006). 24.
7 S. Bishop et al., "Mindfulness: a proposed operational definition," *Clinical Psychology: Science and Practice* 11, no. 3 (2004): 232.

"I make use of my emotions rather than be controlled by them."
"Now that I react more calmly, the people in my team do the same."
"We observe much quicker what is taking place emotionally in our team and do something with it."
"We are better able to distinguish between primary and secondary issues and concentrate better on them."
"We simply take the time and our creativity increases."

Many of the exercises in this book are meditation or yoga exercises and originally come from the East. That immediately raises the question of whether you have to be a Buddhist. The answer is simple: no! Mindfulness makes you clearer and opener in your mind, but rest assured:

- It doesn't empty your mind
- It doesn't make you emotionless
- It doesn't make you withdraw from life
- You won't be striving for enlightenment
- You will still feel pain and discomfort
- You won't be converted to a (new) religion.

This book

The book is about mindful leadership. How you can develop it and how you can use it: for yourself, in teams and in organizations.

In chapter *one* I shall describe the autopilot of leadership, teams and organizations. This is a major pitfall that confronts leaders and it can be difficult to escape from it because we make ourselves immune to change. I will show how, using mindful leadership, which I shall describe in more detail, you really can escape from that autopilot.

Chapter *two* shows in detail what our ability for mindfulness actually is. What it means to regulate your attention and what makes it so interesting to train it and use it. What is the difference between the doing mode and the being mode, and what do rigid and open mindsets look like?

Chapter *three* teaches you the basic skills of mindfulness. There is a description of the basic exercises and you will see how a mindful learning process takes place. On a personal level, it means that you, as manager, learn how to master the game of switching between doing and being. Developing mindfulness makes it possible to adjust how you proportion your attention to what the situation demands: focused in the doing mode and relaxed in the being mode.

In a team on autopilot, attention is quickly narrowed and that leads to a restrictive rather than an open reaction. Objectives become hard targets in a scoring culture; the emotional reality is repressed and not used. Mindful managing of teams is done by creating in your team what I call a *green zone of mindfulness*, which leads to a more harmonious collaboration and better performance. In chapter *four*, I will show you how to organize such a green zone and thus perform with compassion. You shouldn't think that mindfulness is soft or that it doesn't lead to better performance. Quite the opposite: mindful teamwork has a high aspiration level.

With the green zone, you also lay the foundation for directing the organization's attention. I deal with that in chapter *five*. Our focus will not only be on operational excellence but also on issues that demand innovation. How do you deal with developments among your customers and in the social environment which force your organization to change course? Which instruments can you use for this?

In the *closing chapter*, I look at the significance of mastership in mindful leadership.

References

Bishop, S., M. Lau, S. Shapiro, L. Carlson, N. Anderson, and J. Carmody. "Mindfulness: A Proposed Operational Definition." *Clinical Psychology: Science and Practice* 11, no. 3 (2004): 230-41.

Mental Health Foundation. *Be Mindful Report 2010.* Mental Health Foundation, 2010.

Kabat-Zinn, Jon. "Mindfulness-Based Interventions in Context: Past, Present, and Future." *Clinical Psychology: Science and Practice* 10, no. 2 (2003): 144-56.

———. *Waar je ook gaat, daar ben je.* Utrecht: Servire, 2006.

Tan, Chade-Meng. *Search inside Yourself.* New York: HarperCollins, 2012.

TNO. *Arbobalans 2011.* TNO, 2012.

1
The autopilot

"Life is what happens to you while you're busy making other plans."[1]

John Lennon – Beautiful Boy

A lot of managers and leaders are so tied up in enhancing their own performance and that of their teams and organizations that they completely overlook how things are getting out of hand. Suddenly a competitor seizes a large share of the market. Or a business or government body is, much to its surprise, confronted with considerable criticism about its production methods, business ethics or the way it implements policy. Stress and workload in your team remain high and targets are not met – yet again. And, on top of it all, you feel that you are perilously close to a burn-out.

The disappointment is often tangible, for so much has already been invested in improvement processes, culture change, and innovation. And that wasn't a bad idea, for generally managers have a good picture of the challenges facing the organization: performing more effectively and with greater reliability, more intensive teamwork, and adapting to new customer demands and policy needs through innovation.

Despite all good intentions, many organizations apparently have considerable difficulty keeping operational processes in order and

1 Taken from the song Beautiful Boy (Darling Boy) from *Double Fantasy* (1980), the last album John Lennon released before his death.

deploying and maintaining change processes. Again and again, the autopilot of routine takes over and new blind spots arise. Leaders seem unable to focus their own attention and that of their teams and organizations, to see what is really the matter and act accordingly.

In this chapter, I shall sketch – on three levels: organizations, teams, and leaders – how the autopilot works and why it is so persistent. I will show that the core of this mechanism is nothing other than the result of the very human characteristic of trusting in routine. This also occurs, logically enough, when people work together within an organization. And the reason we keep the autopilot alive, even if we see it occasionally, is because we make ourselves immune to change, have a deep internal fear of it. Yet that does not mean you can't change anything – quite the contrary. Mindful leadership, founded on a strong basis of resilience, strengthens our ability to face up to things, including our fear of change, to take responsibility for it, to investigate it and, while innovating, find new ways from a shared perspective. In this way, you can manage both yourself and your teams and organization more effectively.

Organizations: high reliability, innovation, and an open corporate culture

A high level of reliability in processes is expected of many organizations. The examples of this demand for operational excellence are very diverse. They can be surgical teams at hospitals, fire-fighting teams and ambulances, refineries, the back-office of a major bank, or the network of a telecom provider; but they can also be the customer relations department of an insurance company, or city council, or the administrator of the railroad infrastructure. There are two aspects to this high reliability. First, that it is almost always on the cusp of technology and human actions that have to be accurately attuned to each other. Second, and that makes it even more compelling, is that in a number of cases, total reliability is essential. If that is absent, the results can easily be disastrous.[2]

---

2 Karl E. Weick and Kathleen M. Sutcliffe, *Managing the Unexpected* (San Francisco: John Wiley & Sons, 2010). ix.

The railroads can no longer transport thousands of passengers, surgery at a hospital goes wrong with serious consequences for the patient, payment transactions seize up with damaging results for the economy. There are companies and organizations that realize that reliability is their *core business* and know how to act accordingly. What is striking is that they think and act differently, a different culture prevails. One that is characterized by a far greater attentiveness. A sharp perception of matters that deviate from what you expect and the courage to recognize that something must be done. See clearly and not put things off, but signal and intervene. That applies in hospitals and on the deck of an aircraft carrier or for a large banking system, but equally for the customer services department at an internet service provider. You must be highly skilled in the interaction between technology and people to be a modern highly productive organization.

Today, enormous demands are made on our creativity and on the ability of organizations to innovate. Virtually every organization feels the pressure of competition in the market or from policy changes by public authorities. Hospitals face the need to change, as costs rise and patients demand better care. In our societies, innovation is high on the list of priorities because countries must respond to the international call for sustainable renewal. Anybody who looks around will see that many innovation challenges are not restricted to the private sector but affect the public sector as well: climate, water, biodiversity, social inequality, and diversity. And then not only on a national or European level, but on a global level.

Tim Brown, CEO of IDEO – one of the largest design companies in the world – suggests that creativity and innovation require a corporate culture where experimenting, taking risks, and making use of all your creative and human abilities is encouraged. An organizational culture where asking forgiveness in retrospect is valued more than requesting permission in advance. But equally vital is that those cultures are reflective and cooperative. With highly diverse, interdisciplinary teams. Their members must have professional depth and the ability to cooperate across the boundaries of disciplines. Every team member must be able to work from a joint ownership of the ideas and take responsibility for that attitude.[3]

Teams: smarter collaboration through emotional intelligence

Teamwork too is subject to increasingly higher demands. Organizations are restructuring to be better able to create value for customers and stakeholders, to gain or retain market positions, to enter into alliances, or to deal with diversity in society. It means that collaboration increasingly takes place across borders, across teams and departments, but also across companies, public authorities, and other organizations in all sorts of hybrid forms such as alliances or temporary projects. The latest form of this is cloud-based working, in which technological possibilities are combined with the emergence of collaborating in networks.

In addition to expanding across borders, a change in the character of the responsibility for results is visible. It is no longer about individual responsibility for just a part of the activities, a section of the work, but rather about mutual support and shared responsibility for the performance as a whole.

The classic role of the leader as the one who sets the norms, gives direction, and offers security is changing. People in teams play more roles than the official job description would suggest: tasks and roles are increasingly interchangeable. It is no longer the managers who monitor and supervise, but the whole group or team that directs the work and monitors progress.[4]

Both the expansion of collaboration and the shift towards shared responsibility for the results demand smarter forms of collaboration and the use of each other's strengths and competencies. To achieve this, a far stronger appeal is made on the use of emotional intelligence: understanding the emotions of others and being able to deal with them accordingly. Managers must be aware of

3   Tim Brown, *Change by Design* (New York: Harper Collins, 2009). 27-28.
4   Jon R. Katzenbach and Douglas K. Smith, *Het geheim van teams. Een organisatie van wereldklasse creëren* (Schiedam: Scriptum, 1997). 206.

emotions and build a culture of dialogue and effective collaboration.

Leaders: wrestling with change

Organizations invest heavily in performance enhancing programs, culture change, and innovation in order to respond or adjust to the challenges I mentioned earlier. That does not make the manager's task any easier. What problems loom ahead? I will describe them below and also show how exercising mindfulness can help avoid them.

Pitfall 1: Constantly sacrificing yourself

Persistence and perseverance are criteria in the selection of managers, but the pressure of the organization and the willpower and perseverance of the manager himself can be so great that he easily finds himself in a negative spiral of working too much and too hard and taking too little rest. You accept the pain and the inconvenience of the effort required to lead and go on and on.[5] You suppress warning signals: "They simply can't do without me." Or: "If I don't do it, who will?" You keep on sacrificing yourself and this is ultimately at the expense of your own health or the personal relationships with your partner and friends.

If you could detect the danger of stress earlier, you would do yourself a big service. I have noticed that regularly exercising mindfulness sharpens my perception and enables me to react to stress signals sooner and to take appropriate action. Mindfulness also had a much wider effect on my attitude to work: I could pay attention and focus better in my conversations with other people, both at the office and at home. Since then, I have noticed that the quality of my work and the pleasure I have in it has increased and that my attention, when put under pressure, can be more easily redirected. It thus proved possible to escape from the cage of stress and sacrifice, but to do that I had to give up my conviction that I

5 Richard Boyatzis and Annie McKee, *Resonant Leadership* (Cambridge: Harvard Business Press, 2005). 6.

was indispensable. I also had to curb my excessive self-confidence that I could handle anything. Surprisingly enough, when I did this, my resilience turned out to be greater than I had imagined.

Pitfall 2: Focused only on substance

As manager, it's not enough to keep up your resilience. As a matter of fact, that's actually a basic condition, albeit a very important one. Management is, first and foremost, giving day-to-day leadership to teams and developing an effective and productive culture of working in the organization. The challenges are countless. How do you ensure that a team with a wide diversity of characters continues to function well? How do you deal with the many daily decisions and delegating responsibilities? How do you create a culture in which people are players and not victims and in which they can get the best out of themselves?[6] As leader, you are like the spider in the web, keeping all the threads of human relationships in harmony.

Take the example of Karel, a young, successful policy officer at an international development NGO. He was smart and pro-active. His contacts with partners in Latin America went well, because he gave well-founded substantive advice on requests and evaluations of projects, and he didn't mind at all reworking parts of the texts himself at night. When the position of team manager for Latin America became vacant, it was logical that Karel was given the job.

The things Karel did well in the past were repeated here: quick contact with his employees and an emphasis on substance. There was a lot to do, because the position had been vacant for some time. A backlog in project assessments and evaluations had to be cleared away. And at the same time, a change in direction at the ministry of development aid meant that a policy change had to be implemented. The number of partners in Latin America had to be considerably reduced, even cut back to zero in three countries. Colleagues who tried to share their stories and emotions about the consequences of these changes with Karel found his door closed to

6 Fred Kofman, *Bewust in zaken* (Haarlem: Altamira-Becht, 2008). From 50.

them. The content of the case was completely in order and that was all that mattered to him.

Until a very dissatisfied and shocked letter from the Latin American partners landed on the director's desk *and* – almost at the same time – the team lodged a complaint with the head of HR about Karel's leadership because he showed not the least bit of interest in his people.

When both matters were discussed in a meeting between Karel and the director, something snapped: "This can't be true! I've put all my energy into it." Apparently the need to get content and practical issues right had been Karel's priority over giving any attention to emotional reality. His team felt completely left out in the cold, and so did the partners with whom they worked.

Fortunately, Karel proved very resilient. He realized that he had continued working as team manager in the same way he had done previously as policy officer. Together with his director, he visited the Latin American partners to discuss the new policy with them and the changes this would entail. In his team, he had personal meetings with his employees, and these cleared the air.

But he also realized he would have to keep on training himself in being attentive to the emotional reality and the nature of the culture in his team. And he did just that. He nurtured an attitude of attention and thus learned how to pick up on signals much earlier. He learned to recognize emotions and give them space, although he had to let go of his idea that emotions were, above all, obstructive. And he took time for much more personal contact with his team. It prevented problems from escalating. He discovered to his amazement that by paying friendly attention, there was a much better balance and greater energy in his team.

What Karel experienced with his team also works in maintaining the relationships that an organization has with the outside world. Depending on the sort of organization, this can involve a wide variety of people, groups, and stakeholders. We can even extend it from emotions to being attentive to physical and mental signals in general. I have already written about the challenge that certain teams face, such as surgical or fire-fighting teams, which must operate faultlessly and reliably under high pressure. It is then crucial to use all your senses to observe every possible signal. A light physical sensation in a leg or arm, a strange feeling or an intuition can set you on the track towards something that could prove dangerous or which must be corrected. In other words, in every case it is essential not only to watch substance, but also to remain connected with the emotional reality.

For that you must have the courage to acknowledge things and name them. And to take steps to do things differently. Mindfulness also trains that courage and enables teams and their leaders to deal more intelligently with each other, because it increases their emotional intelligence and their ability to work together in a smart and relaxed way.

Pitfall 3: Sticking to certainties

Good leadership in a situation of intentional change demands that leaders be capable of looking outside and inside with an open mind, that they dare to ask questions beyond the boundaries of their own limitations. And they must be capable of articulating new values and concepts and of involving their team or company in solving its dilemmas of strategy and organizational culture.

Edgar Schein provides a detailed description of a change project at Ciba-Geigy in the 1980s (the company has since merged with Sandoz to form Novartis) in which these roles were carried out with drive and rewarded with success.[7] Ciba-Geigy had a strong science-geared culture with a clear hierarchy. A number of divisions were under-performing but that problem was casually brushed aside because the company as a whole was in the black. The problem, however, emerged at a large leadership conference during a comparison of the figures by division. Considerable concern and uncertainty were the result.

The leadership team (around fifty people) at Ciba-Geigy succeeded in implementing a renewal of the organization. The disquiet that arose when it emerged that the company wasn't doing as well as was thought, was addressed through a renewal program

7 Edgar H. Schein, *Organizational Culture and Leadership* (San Francisco: Jossey Bass, 2010). 339-62.

that included horizontal communications and clearly managed task groups. Restrictive hierarchy and rigid thought structures were abandoned. That the CEO of the company, Sam Koechlin, was the first to be able to make the switch proved the crux of the change process. He could apply the attention and the perception to see what was happening and was able to accept that his image of reality was inaccurate. At the same time, the strength of the program was that a number of cultural certainties the organization had, such as well-founded knowledge and clear collaboration, were carried over to the new way of working. In this way, the good was retained and the impediments of the old working method were removed.

Another example. For a drinks manufacturer such as Coca-Cola, use of water is essential and for years they have concentrated on using water as efficiently as possible at each bottling plant. But gradually, they became aware that there was a broader responsibility. Coca-Cola would, whether they liked it or not, be held responsible for the sustainable development of the water systems. Coca-Cola chose to enter into an alliance with the World Wildlife Fund. WWF helped Coca-Cola to ascertain where the water used in the company actually originated, far beyond the local authority. And gradually the focus switched from concentrating on water efficiency to concentrating on the "water footprint" of the company, in which water used for other ingredients, such as the cultivation of cane sugar, was included.[8] Both Coca-Cola and WWF had to discard old prejudices and step over their boundaries. That was something in the mindset of the employees of both companies, and what helped was that they discovered that behind an old opponent, there was often an interesting human being. But it also emerged that the definition of each organization's own business – "efficiently producing soft drinks" or "saving nature" – proved a lot broader than it was initially thought.

8 Peter Senge et al., *The Necessary Revolution* (New York: Doubleday, 2008). 77-95.

The autopilot keeps taking over

The examples of the struggles of the leaders discussed above, whether they were personal, with their teams, or with their organizations, ultimately turned out fairly well. But the examples of managers who continue to work too hard with all the consequences this has for their personal life and for the teams they lead are legion.

The reason things so often go wrong when we, as leaders, instigate change is because we do not really fully understand the challenge we are facing. We often approach them as a familiar technical problem and try to solve them with a "quick fix" that worked on previous occasions or some other standard technique, without really having a clear idea of what is really the matter. Karel first tried it by concentrating on substance, which was a familiar area for him. My own approach was to improve my physical condition, for I thought I would then encounter fewer problems from the stress and the exhaustion, yet the opposite proved true. Coca-Cola had tried on various occasions to solve its water problems by drawing up exclusive water contracts with the local authorities; the result was resistance from and rebellion by the local population.

If we put our faith in the familiar technical solution, it apparently doesn't work.

In many cases, leaders of organizations are confronted with challenges that cannot be addressed with standard solutions. The challenges are too diverse, too new and they are often in unknown territory. That is why we call them "adaptive" challenges. And these cannot be solved by adding an extra set of competencies to your current ones. You can only address this type of challenge if you are prepared to undergo a mental development, to change your mindset. Change is not only about the problem itself, but also about the person facing the problem.[9]

And it is exactly at this point that the autopilot of routine so easily kicks in. Let us therefore take a look at this autopilot to see what it looks like and why it is so stubborn.

9 Ronald Heifetz, Alexander Grashow, and Martin Linsky, *The Practice of Adaptive Leadership* (Boston: Harvard Business Press, 2009). 19.

The power of habit

In one of our training sessions, a participant told us about an injury he had suffered to his arm. After taking a shower, he noticed that he had suddenly lost the whole routine of how to dry himself. He always did it without thinking and now he didn't know what to do.

With the autopilot on a personal level, we impose restrictions on our thinking and on our action repertoire from the context in which we operate; we create a fixed mindset. That gives us a comprehensive view and clarity. In addition, routines provide certainty and familiarity, and make it easier to get along with each other.

But in this power of certainty there lurks a pitfall: the power of habit.[10] For in the standard situation we quickly assume that things are what they are and therefore miss the signals that contradict them and which could encourage us to alertness or change. Then our perception lacks clarity, and as a consequence we find ourselves in an unpleasant or damaging situation, such as over-exhaustion or lack of attention to our team. The power of habit also makes us want to cling to the existing state: it is fine the way it is, we are satisfied with it. We turn away from the necessary change, because we'd rather not begin it.

Blind to new facts

In organizations too we see the mechanism of the autopilot in action. In his most recent book, Chris Argyris, together with Donald Schön, the father of the theory of organizational learning,[11] gives a somewhat gloomy summary of the state: we keep falling into pitfalls. Even though we sometimes have a good picture in organizations of how we operate, the theory about it in our minds and in our words (he calls that the "theory espoused") is different from the one we demonstrate in practice (the "theory-in-use").

10 For this, please see a fine reference work: Charles Duhigg, *Macht der gewoonte* (Amsterdam: Ambo, 2012).
11 Chris Argyris, *Organizational Traps* (Oxford: Oxford University Press, 2010).

Organizational cultures develop as an answer to external or internal challenges, such as a new technology that becomes available or the necessity to find new customers for products or services, and then enjoy a period of considerable effectiveness. But after a while, familiarity creeps in and the answers given to customer demands become increasingly routine. A mental model develops which becomes a fixed value and the underlying assumptions for this are no longer visible or known.

That becomes a problem once the circumstances change. The model of the iceberg is a good metaphor for this.[12] When confronted with new circumstances, whether internal or external, the standard answer no longer proves to work. The team has become blind and only sees the part of the iceberg that is above water, not the assumptions under water that prevent an adequate reaction to the new circumstances. In almost all cases it seems that people first avoid the new reality or will not face new facts. And when that is not enough, a defense mechanism takes over. "That can't be true, that research is simply wrong!"

Often people and organizations react to awkward matters with the attitude of "notch it up a bit," take a few additional steps. Sometimes that provides some short-term gain, but if that becomes the organization's standard response, it reinforces the blindness to new circumstances and leads to a pattern that is not effective.

Fear of change

It is not only difficult to recognize the autopilot in time and to disengage it: we actually want to keep it in operation. We see that in the defense reaction I described above. Robert Kegan and Lisa Lahey call that our immunity to change, which is a reaction to our fear for it.[13] A mechanism goes into operation in people, and so also in the organizations, with which we react to effort, discomfort, new information or awkward situations. That mechanism has the aim of maximizing our security in order to keep our fear under

12 Peter Senge, *De vijfde discipline* (Schiedam: Scriptum, 1992). From 170.
13 Robert Kegan and Lisa Laskow Lahey, *Immunity to Change* (Cambridge: Harvard Business Press, 2009).

control. The power of this is that it deeply affects our feelings and experiences, it mobilizes our fear for change. It makes us want to keep hold of the safe, the existing and preferably suppress the unsafe, the new. And exactly when we enter the unknown field of adaptive change, that mechanism operates even stronger. Because there it means that we will have to change personally too and the fear even becomes bigger then. The autopilot gets a strong impulse because of this.

Leadership in unknown territory

Agreeable work with less stress, higher reliability of operational processes, much more extensive teamwork with horizontal responsibilities and a greater call for creativity and innovation. It is always about adaptive problems for which there is no clear and defined solution (for then we would have already applied it).[14] And yet modern organizations – and they can be companies, public authorities, or non-profit organizations – want to create value for their customers and at the same time for their social environment. There are two demands on leadership in unknown territory. First, it must be capable of helping the team or the organization to understand exactly what is happening while the uncertainty about it is great. And second, it must be capable of disengaging the autopilot and breaking down the immunity to change. What does leadership look like and what role does mindfulness play in it?

Directing attention

Edgar Schein, grandmaster of cultural change and leadership in organizations, states in the most recent edition of his standard work about organizational culture that leadership that takes organizations and society further must meet a number of conditions.[15] To start with, he states, leaders must be able to understand and develop insight into the circumstances. For that, they must develop the skills of "humble inquiry": acknowledging what is and

14 Heifetz, Grashow, and Linsky, *The Practice of Adaptive Leadership.*
15 Schein, *Organizational Culture and Leadership*: 380-83.

investigating it without any prior certainties and, when doing this, assuming the attitude of "not knowing the answer" and admitting to not having it under control. They must have the courage to question and untie matters, even if that causes discomfort and anxiety. They must possess emotional strength to bear the anxiety of the changes in the organization. And they must be capable of allowing the group to participate in finding new paths, in the cognitive redefinition of the existing organizational culture. The new reality must after all be a reality that is jointly created and supported.

His approach to leadership deviates from others who place the emphasis on taking decisions, managing the planning and control cycle or the personal attitude (serving or authentic) of the leader, but emphasizes the fact that leadership is relational. Management and leadership are about relating to employees and a leader cannot exist without good followers. Together they make the movement of the group, as shown in an interesting clip on YouTube.[16] As leader, you cannot nowadays really take any decision from a purely hierarchical position. Your authority has become ambiguous and you can only get people to do things if they want to do it themselves. That means that you must have much more attention for emotions and must be skilful in dealing with them.[17]

In addition to the ability to resonate with followers, there is another aspect that leaders have to take into account. When work takes place beyond the borders of one's own organization and in different time zones, managers no longer have the only formal and factual responsibility for leading people and achieving results. In such teams, a lot more people have a leading or directing role. And so increasingly there is joint or collective leadership. That particularly applies to situations in which major complex social matters have to be addressed. Leadership is then no longer about "me" but

16 Video from YouTube: http://www.youtube.com/watch?v=GA8z7f7a2Pk (visited on 6 June 2012 at 14.50). At the Sasquatch! Music Festival, a boy begins to dance, without any effect. Only when a follower joins in does a real movement emerge.

17 Boyatzis and McKee, *Resonant Leadership*: 182.

about "us." Every manager faces the dilemma of whether to direct his energy from the question "what do I want" or from "what does the situation demand of me" and that is a crucial choice. It is about not imposing your own idea or solution on others, a form of egocentric or macho leadership, but if you are prepared to investigate with others what is needed, thus a more serving and supportive leadership.

Building on this, Otto Scharmer, in his book *Theory U* suggests that leadership is about the question of how you can increase the capacity of people, teams, and organizations within a system to see fully the reality they are dealing with and within which they must operate. To discover and develop the power of seeing and seeing together.[18]

Here leadership is not just about managing and directing; allocating duties and control are fine but insufficient. It is also more than stating a vision and setting the course. For that puts finding the direction or the solution primarily with the leaders, while we have just seen that leadership is increasingly a joint process. It is all about ensuring that the collective attention is directed on the here and now and, when necessary, on what is emerging. Ensuring that the awareness of what "we" are doing is widely present.

Mindfulness on the rise

Mindfulness as a term may only have entered our vocabulary in recent years, but it is not new. We know it as "attention" or "awareness" and recognize it as a characteristic that everybody has in his nature. Even more, it is part of that which makes us human: our ability to be fully conscious, to be aware of everything that takes place in ourselves and in our environment.[19]

As a term, mindfulness originally appeared in old Buddhist texts. In Pali, the language in which many of Buddha's speeches

18 C. Otto Scharmer, *Theorie U. Leiding vanuit de toekomst die zich aandient* (Zeist: Christofoor, 2010). 176.

19 Ronald D. Siegel, Christopher K. Germer, and Andrew Olendzki, "Mindfulness: What Is It? Where Did It Come From?," in *Clinical Handbook of Mindfulness*, ed. Fabrizio Didonna (New York: Springer, 2009). 17.

are written, the word *sati* – mindfulness – stands for awareness, attention, and remembering. Consciousness and attention are terms that suggest a certain capacity or ability. With conscious attention to what takes place around us, we begin to free ourselves of fuss, of preoccupations, of awkward emotions, and space arises in thinking and acting. "Remembering" is not about a type of memory function or accessing your personal hard disk of the past. No, it is about realizing what you are doing, a tiny bell that rings: "don't forget to be aware." It refers to the intention of being attentive.

Mindfulness begins with how you as manager deal with your own attention, but we can also view it from the perspective of organizations. Then we talk of the quality of awareness in the organization. Routines and roles are built into every organization. You know what you must do and what you can expect of each other. The advantage here is that activities are predictable and cost relatively little mental energy. That is handy. But fixed patterns also have a reverse side: they cause blind spots because they prevent you from noticing things in good time, endangering the execution. Mindfulness in organizations means that there is a richer awareness. That starts with noticing details that make a difference. The importance of this should not be underestimated because it is crucial when people must perform under pressure. Exactly then, our inclination to allow only confirming information into our awareness is greater than when the pressure is absent.[20] Mindfulness means that small errors or deviations are noticed and are not reasoned away. Mindfulness prevents simplification and reinforces conscious acting. So that an adjustment can be found well in advance.

But by noticing more consciously what is happening, you subsequently also strengthen the possibilities of the organization to direct attention at developments from the environment and you create more openness and space for innovations. Mindfulness in organizations begins by directing attention at what is happening here and now. For even though you are well experienced as a manager and even if you have a lot of wonderful plans for the future,

20 Weick and Sutcliffe, *Managing the Unexpected*: 23.

what is decisive is what is taking place here and now.[21] And that extends to what is coming into existence.

In the last twenty years, extensive research has been carried out into the effects of exercising mindfulness. A number of important issues have emerged from this, and I shall deal with them further in chapter two. A few examples of effects: a larger processing capacity in the brain and therefore higher quality in decision-making, greater resilience and better stress handling, strengthened emotional intelligence and, from there, better collaboration with others, a more acute eye for the social environment. In essence, mindfulness helps you learn how you can mentally switch your attention. You develop a greater presence of mind and as a manager you can use this to direct your team or organization in a far better way.

The power of mindful leadership

Leadership that makes maximum use of this ability for mindfulness is an important way of escaping the autopilot and of combating the immunity to change. That is possible because, as we shall discuss in detail in the following chapter, we learn to switch mentally between action and reflection, between doing and being. Such leadership is capable of addressing adaptive problems, the wrestling with changes in an unknown territory. That is because mindful leadership disengages the autopilot and combats the mechanism that makes us immune to change, by changing our way of looking, experiencing, and giving meaning. It helps us to be awake and enables us to acknowledge experiences and investigate them, before interpreting them.[22] In this way, our mind, with all our experiences, becomes a tool that we can use instead of it forcing us towards a certain perception and interpretation. We learn to free ourselves from the autopilot and to choose a conscious response. That demands courage: a certain intrepidity to address your fear for change and to accept that it is there. Such a mind is

21 Ibid., 32-33.
22 Kegan and Lahey, *Immunity to Change*: 53.

not only capable of forming a new picture of how the organization must work and generating the courage to continue to follow this course. That mind is also capable of stepping out of its own fixed mindset, recognizing its limitations and developing a new, more all-embracing mindset. A leader who dares to switch between action and reflection and a mind that has the courage to transform itself. Reflection in action.

I therefore define mindful leadership as follows: *consciously experiencing both the internal and external world and from this, directing the attention of individuals and groups at a situation and what it demands of you and them.* Such leadership based on mindfulness has a number of dimensions. The training of our ability for mindfulness affects each of these dimensions. Together they make mindful leadership a powerful tool.

To start with, it strengthens **resilience** in leaders. Resilience means that our physical and mental fighting spirit is kept in good condition and continuously renewed and tended. This resilience enables you to bear pressure and anxiety in the organization when that proves necessary. Resilience means taking responsibility for your own well-being and being alert to signals that could indicate hidden exhaustion. Taking your own limitations seriously and acting accordingly.

Next, mindfulness strengthens the capacity for a **fearless presence of mind**. That means being present without any reservation with what there is, addressing the facts, including ones that are painful, awkward or that have been avoided in the past. Pausing, the "humble inquiry" of Schein, is the first element in this, acknowledging what there is, and accepting the situation and taking that as the starting point.

The following element is having the courage to be present and to stay with the discomfort and the uncertainty, with the fear and anxiety that can be generated. And doing that not only to yourself, but also doing the same with the team or organization you lead, sharing their fear and anxiety.

The courage to have presence of mind builds upon resilience

and in turn strengthens it. Fearless presence of mind, rooted in resilience, is, in my opinion, the core of leadership based on mindfulness. That it takes such a central position is because of its role in
recognizing and investigating experiences and the importance it
has in being able to handle the anxiety of others and the courage to
take the required action. It is the crucial factor in combating immunity towards change.

Mindfulness also strengthens taking *unconditional responsibility*. It means taking responsibility for the situation, however difficult. I call that, together with Kofman, unconditional, because in
every case you have the ability to react to a situation and not to allow your reaction to be determined by external circumstances or
your instinct. You choose to be a player and not a victim.[23]

Victor Frankl's attitude to life during his internment in the German concentration camps has, in a special way, become a symbol
for this. He was able to shift his attitude to life consciously from
the question "what do I want to happen?" to one of "what does this
situation ask of me?" thus embodying the hope for a better future.[24] Frankl made clear that even if you are unable to determine
the circumstances, you still have the freedom to make the choice
of how to deal with them. He was even able, under the most difficult circumstances, to comfort and help others and to keep alight
the spark of humanity and a belief in a better world.

And that is what is expected of leadership. The attitude shifts
from your own interests to an attitude that takes the whole as its
starting point, the "we" position. Leaders are then capable of directing the attention of a group differently, by example, by facili-
tating processes, by giving direction and instructions.

What mindfulness further embodies for leadership is *enquiring
openness*. Investigating experiences and patterns in the culture –

---

23 Kofman, *Bewust in zaken*: 52-54. Kofman's understanding of unconditional responsibility is based on the incredible story of Victor Frankl in
the concentration camps in the Second World War. See: Victor Frankl,
Man's Search for Meaning (Boston: Beacon Press, 2006). 75.
24 *Man's Search for Meaning*.

often internalized – and letting go of them, no longer identifying yourself with them. In combination with fearlessness, this means breaking down, where necessary, existing patterns, making existing relationships "defrost." In order to do that, you must act honestly and retain that integrity in difficult circumstances.[25] And you must be prepared to learn from that. Investigative openness enables you to see the mechanism of the autopilot which either makes you stick with the familiar or makes you recoil from the unknown.

And finally, training our ability for mindfulness reinforces leaders' capacity for *experimental, innovative and connecting action,*[26] with which they direct the attention of the organizations or the wider system in which they operate onto that which is unfolding before them. Bringing about the shift from the existing to the new, from a closed mindset to an open one. From attention for the technical to attention for adaptive problems. With an attitude that no longer reasons from the "I" but from the "we."

Leadership based on mindfulness makes itself felt in various areas: in learning to know and care for yourself, in the development of a personal vision, the courage to show leadership, in coaching of individual employees, in the building of organizational cultures that recognize mindfulness as a fundamental attitude, and in leadership towards the outside world. That is the power of attention and fearless presence. In the following chapters we will show what this ability for mindfulness is, how you can develop it and apply it in managing teams and leading organizations.

References

Argyris, Chris. *Organizational Traps*. Oxford: Oxford University Press, 2010.

Boyatzis, Richard, and Annie McKee. *Resonant Leadership*. Cambridge: Harvard Business Press, 2005.

Brown, Tim. *Change by Design*. New York: Harper Collins, 2009.

Duhigg, Charles. *Macht der gewoonte*. Amsterdam: Ambo, 2012.

Frankl, Victor. *Man's Search for Meaning*. Boston: Beacon Press, 2006.

Heifetz, Ronald, Alexander Grashow, and Martin Linsky. *The Practice of Adaptive Leadership*. Boston: Harvard Business Press, 2009.

Katzenbach, Jon R., and Douglas K. Smith. *Het geheim van teams. Een organisatie van wereldklasse creëren*. Schiedam: Scriptum, 1997.

Kegan, Robert, and Lisa Laskow Lahey. *Immunity to Change*. Cambridge: Harvard Business Press, 2009.

Kofman, Fred. *Bewust in zaken*. Haarlem: Altamira-Becht, 2008.

Scharmer, C. Otto. *Theorie U. Leiding vanuit de toekomst die zich aandient*. Zeist: Christofoor, 2010.

Schein, Edgar H. *Organizational Culture and Leadership*. San Francisco: Jossey Bass, 2010.

Senge, Peter. *De vijfde discipline*. Schiedam: Scriptum, 1992.

Senge, Peter, Bryan Smith, Nina Kruschwitz, Joe Laur, and Sara Schley. *The Necessary Revolution*. New York: Doubleday, 2008.

Siegel, Ronald D., Christopher K. Germer, and Andrew Olendzki. "Mindfulness: What Is It? Where Did It Come From?". In *Clinical Handbook of Mindfulness*, edited by Fabrizio Didonna. 17-35. New York: Springer, 2009.

Weick, Karl E., and Kathleen M. Sutcliffe. *Managing the Unexpected*. San Francisco: John Wiley & Sons, 2010.

2
Mindfulness: doing and being

"When cultivated and refined, mindfulness can function effectively on every level, from the individual to the corporate, the societal, the political, and the global. But it does require that we be motivated to realize who we actually are and to live our lives as if they really mattered, not just for ourselves, but for the world. This adventure of a lifetime unfolds from this first step."[1]

Jon Kabat-Zinn – *Coming to Our Senses*

After the description of mindful leadership as directing the individual and collective attention at what the situation demands of us, I shall, in this chapter, discuss what exactly our ability for mindfulness is and how it works. With mindfulness as a form of conscious attention, you learn how to switch mentally between action and reflection, between what we, in mindfulness training, call doing and being.

Mindfulness is part of the way our body-mind system regulates itself and the relationship with its surroundings. This is an extremely useful system, but it can malfunction if you continue to operate on autopilot. Then your balance can be lost, with all the negative consequences for yourself in the form of stress or burnout, or for your team that could find itself in the rut of no longer adequate cultural patterns.

Fortunately, we can train mindfulness. To show you how to do this, I will let you see how mindfulness works: you take the experience as a starting point and approach it with attentiveness. I shall sketch the working mechanism of mindfulness and indicate which attitude is necessary to train that attentiveness.

I close the chapter by showing how you can set to work with mindfulness: directing the attention. And how you can learn to use

1   Jon Kabat-Zinn, *Coming to Our Senses* (New York: Hyperion, 2005). 11.

that mental switching between action and reflection for yourself, for team management, and for organizational development.

Mindfulness: what it is

A superficial self-analysis quickly shows us that we are, with great regularity, in a state of inattentiveness and thoughtlessness. The examples are numerous: the highway exit that you miss and the small mishaps in everyday things such as shaving or cutting cheese. Or you are in a meeting that is scheduled to last an hour and after ten minutes you think: "Uhm, still another 50 minutes of this." What is being said at that moment escapes you. Our mind is somewhere out there, our body here.

If you pay careful attention, you realize that our mind is absent for a large part of the time or our thoughts are rushing backwards and forwards in time. Thinking about the past and what happened or what is coming and which may prove difficult for us. Disagreeable experiences are pushed as far away as possible. You are not in the here and now, and we call that mind*less*.

Our whole life is, to a large extent, based on lengthy repetition and exercise of activities that have become so self-evident that we forget how they actually take place. Just ask an NBA star how he manages three-pointer after three-pointer. Almost certainly he won't be able to give you an answer. Routine isn't bad, it is also an expression of skill.

Another habit is how easily we attach importance to a first impression, without looking further. Our body-mind system can be easily deceived and that quickly leads to confusion or lack of clarity. Take "blindness to change." There are clips on YouTube, based on research that shows how badly we observe things: the test subject is having a conversation with man A. Two men pass by with a plank of wood – man A disappears and his place is quickly taken by man B. The test person does *not* realize that a new person has taken the place of man A, and he simply keeps the conversation going.[2]

2 J. Mark G. Williams and Jon Kabat-Zinn, "Mindfulness: Diverse Perspectives on Its Meaning, Origins, and Multiple Applications at the Intersection of Science and Dharma," *Contemporary Buddhism* 12, no. 1 (2011): 16.

A final limitation arises from the context in which we operate.[3] In a divorce, for example, it often revolves around the question of who "gets" the children. But what is that "get" exactly? What is at stake here? The physical presence of the child, a certain relationship of care toward the child? Could it be about getting love from the child, or even the satisfaction of taking revenge? Regularly the question of the children is seen as a "zero-sum-game." Which it isn't, of course. For children are perfectly capable of loving both parents, irrespective of whom they live with. And the reverse is also true: parents can love their children even if they live with the other parent. The limited context is the idea that love and care are scarce resources, for which we must fight: if I get more, you get less.

In organizations too we witness a lot of mindlessness, habit patterns. People operate according to a formula, the jokes with colleagues are the same each day. Based on organizational culture, our mind interprets everything within the existing categories and new experiences are – incorrectly – placed in familiar pigeon holes.[4]

The autopilot is useful, you can do things skillfully and with a limited degree of mental effort. But the downside is that an excess of routine operation hinders your ability to act attentively, openly, creatively, and innovatively. And that is exactly what is expected of leadership.

Jon Kabat-Zinn, founder of mindfulness training in its current form, describes mindfulness as *"paying attention in a particular way: on purpose, in the present moment, and non-judgmentally."*[5] It is all about a conscious activity: paying attention and observing what arises, nothing more. We shall describe these three elements – attention, consciousness, and non-judgmental – in detail later.

This being observant, the state of mindfulness, allows you to observe your feelings or thoughts as events in the mind, without

3   Ellen Langer, *Mindfulness* (Cambridge: Perseus, 1989). 31-40.
4   Karl E. Weick and Kathleen M. Sutcliffe, *Managing the Unexpected* (San Francisco: John Wiley & Sons, 2010). 88.
5   Jon Kabat-Zinn, *Waar je ook gaat, daar ben je* (Utrecht: Servire, 2006). 24.

strongly associating yourself with them and without reacting in a familiar automatic pattern. This calm way of reacting gives rise to a moment of space between observation and response. And so mindfulness makes it possible for you to provide a more thoughtful answer to a situation instead of a reflex.[6]

Buddhist origins

Mindfulness originally arose from the Buddhist tradition. In Pali, the language in which many of Buddha's speeches are written, it is described as *sati* and that stands for awareness, attention, and remembering. Consciousness and attention are terms that suggest a certain capacity or ability. With conscious attention for what presents itself to us, we begin to free ourselves of fuss, of preoccupations, of awkward emotions, and space arises in thinking and acting.

The third aspect "remembering" is often neglected, yet it is an important element of mindfulness. "Remembering" is not about a type of memory function or accessing your personal hard disk of the past. No, it is about realizing what you are doing, a tiny bell that rings: "don't forget to be aware." It refers to the intention to be attentive: remembering you are in the present moment, in the here and now.

It is interesting that Freud, the founder of psychoanalysis, also mentioned the importance of that process. After he had distanced himself from the approach in which he brought his patients under hypnosis, he placed his confidence in the free association of thoughts. He called that "studying the current psychic surface of the person under analysis." He placed, just like the Buddha, the emphasis on the importance of attentiveness to the experiences in the here and now. The difference between these two is that Freud restricted this process of observation to the hours on a psychoanalyst's couch, while the Buddha taught that observance could have a much wider operation, throughout the day in all our activities.[7]

6 S. Bishop et al, "Mindfulness: A Proposed Operational Definition," *Clinical Psychology: Science and Practice* 11, no. 3 (2004): 232.

7 Mark Epstein, *Gedachten zonder denker. Psychotherapie vanuit boeddhistisch perspectief* (Rotterdam: Asoka, 2007). 175-76.

State and process

In modern clinical psychology, the core process of mindfulness is described using two components. The first is allowing the attention to rest on the immediate experience and thus allow recognition of those mental experiences in the current moment. Thereby, and that is the second component, we adopt after these experiences a certain attitude that can be characterized as an attitude of curiosity, openness, and acceptance.[8]

Mindfulness seems to be a state, but it is simultaneously a process. The state is that of "*being consciously present*." In the process, the emphasis is on "*consciously directing the attention*" onto what is happening now. It appears as if that state cannot easily be maintained. We cannot constantly be in the state of complete awareness, it is more about a coming and going of moments.

Fortunately we know that human abilities, such as running, dancing, or thinking, can be trained. And that is also true of mindfulness, as is shown by nearly thirty years of scientific study into the effects of mindfulness, but also by the 2500 year old tradition of Buddhist psychology. By training the conscious direction of our awareness with the help of our attentiveness, we strengthen our ability for mindfulness and we can maintain the state of presence of mind for longer. In the following chapter I will deal in greater depth with the training of the basic skills.

Organizations and mindfulness

We can also view mindfulness from the perspective of organizations. In organizations, behavior is embodied in routines, roles, and strategies. You can rely on the other to act in accordance with the expected pattern associated with a routine or a role. That has both advantages and disadvantages. The advantage is that activities can be carried out predictably and with relatively little mental energy. If you satisfy the expectations associated with your role, whether you are an employee or a manager in an organization,

8 S. Bishop et al., "Mindfulness: A Proposed Operational Definition," *Clinical Psychology*.

you can be virtually certain that things will run as they should. That is handy. But routines and roles also have a reverse side: they cause blind spots because they prevent you from noticing in time things that can endanger the planned execution. Or the limitations of the current context mean that an organization is not open to new developments, which prevents the timely development of a new strategy.

To combat this, organizations must develop a richer awareness. That, too, is mindfulness and its importance must not be underestimated. On the one hand, it is crucial because it is exactly when we are under pressure that our inclination to allow only confirming information into our awareness is greater than when the pressure is absent.[9] On the other hand, because it is important to be open to entering unknown territory and capable of observing the wide periphery of the organization when effectuating a new direction.

In this context, you can describe mindfulness as a rich insight into differentiating characteristics, in which people, while working, are conscious of the context in which they are operating, of the way in which details differ from each other and of the way in which what they observe differs from what they expect. They have an overview of the larger whole, even if that is the whole of that moment. This is also called situational awareness, but that is a rather static description, and mindfulness distinguishes itself from that because it is a constant process of observing and distinguishing.[10] It is therefore also open toward the future.

Mindfulness in organizations is thus about the quality of the attention, just as it is on a personal level. That works best if everybody in the organization "keeps his mind on the job," is mindful. We expect leaders to monitor the organizational attention and give it direction, even now when leadership is increasingly shared with a team. Day-to-day management is primarily directed at working attentively in the here and now, strategic leadership is more about exploring the unknown territory of the future.

Mindfulness from this perspective begins by directing the organization at observing and recognizing what is happening here

9 Weick and Sutcliffe, *Managing the Unexpected*: 23.
10 Ibid., 32.

and now. For even though you may have considerable experience as a manager and have wonderful plans for the future, what is decisive is what is taking place here and now.[11] You could see it as teaching an organization to adopt a careful but at the same time relaxed observation ability.[12] *Presence of mind* is an antidote against ingrained patterns in organizations and in the society in which we live.

Mentally switching attention

What you learn in mindfulness training is to observe your own mental experiences and thus not get stuck in these habitual patterns. You make room for switching from doing mode to being mode and back again. That is called mental switching.[13] Your attention is on the constant process of experiences presenting themselves to you and you have your hand on the gear stick to shift gears. You free yourself of the habitual interpretations of your experiences and create space for new insights.

In order to see how this mental switching between action and reflection, between doing and being, works, it is handy to briefly contemplate how mindfulness is part of our entire body-mind system. Then we will discuss the two positions of mental switching – doing and being.

Mindfulness and our body-mind system

The first way of looking at mental switching and how it is embedded in our body-mind system is from the perspective of stress. Because you react to stress in two ways: via the autopilot of the unconscious physiological reaction or by the conscious response from mindfulness. When you experience stress, an immediate physiological reaction occurs in your body. Your hormonal sys-

11 Ibid., 32-33.
12 Frits Koster, *Bevrijdend inzicht* (Rotterdam: Asoka, 1999). 99.
13 Zindel V. Segal, J. Mark G. Williams, and John D. Teasdale, *Aandachtgerichte cognitieve therapie bij depressie* (Amsterdam: Uitgeverij Nieuwezijds, 2006). 69-70.

tem takes over to ensure that your body is capable of reacting to the threatening situation. Your physical energy is mobilized and you can fight, flee, or freeze. At earlier stages in the evolution of man, it was an exceptionally sensible reaction involving life and death. Today, the direct threat of death in our society is less – fortunately – but the body does not make a distinction between physical and psychological threats or between threats from inside or outside and still reacts to moments of stress. Worrying about your health or your relationship, about your work, about how your company or organization is functioning, about your own role as manager. It all leads to stress. The mind is constantly assessing whether the situation is safe or threatening. If there is a suggestion of threat, the body is put on alert. Once it is safe again, the body receives signals that it can relax.[14] The conscious reaction from mindfulness helps us to achieve that state of relaxation. In this way, a broader view on what is happening arises.

The second, somewhat more recent but no less interesting way (they are, by the way, not mutually exclusive), is to link the mental switching with the newest insights in the functioning of our brain. Directing our attention, by pausing and observing with openness, in the view of neuro-psychiatrist Daniel Siegel, has the power to influence the functioning of our brain.[15] That is because our mind is an integral part of our body. The mind is a regulating process, in which streams of energy and information are transmitted, monitored, and given direction. That occurs in the spot where we normally place our mental life, in the brains and in the neural networks associated with it. But also in the rest of the body, for the neural networks that process information and energy are everywhere, in our heart, and intestines, and in our immune system. Moreover, we must understand that our mind is a process that is in contact with the environment. The energy and information flows between and among people; it is a mutual exchange. Goleman calls this the open loop of our limbic system that regulates

14 Jon Kabat-Zinn, *Handboek meditatief ontspannen* (Haarlem: Altamira-Becht, 2004). From 264.
15 J. Daniel Siegel, *Mindsight. The New Science of Personal Transformation* (New York: Bantam Books, 2010). 54-55.

our emotions in relationship to our environment.[16] In short, our body-mind system is not only concerned about itself but is also capable of continuous exchange with the environment. And that is precisely the basis that supports the process of directing our attention.

Both insights – that of the stress system and of the brain – teach us that in our body-mind system we have the possibilities of reacting consciously without being completely bound to our physiological reactions. We are capable of conscious response to situations and that can create space between impulse and action, leading to a more open mind. And in this way we can make choices instead of displaying reflexes. Our attention or attentiveness plays a central role in switching or balancing our body-mind system. By shifting our attention (and not wanting to control or suppress emotions, thoughts or experiences), we can better regulate what we think and feel and that is a crucial capability for managers. The result is that space arises for new insights and conscious choosing. "Learn to think what you want to think" is not without reason the title of an introductory book about Buddhism by Dutch Zen teacher Rients Ritskes.[17]

In mindfulness training, the mental switching with our attention is sub-divided into two modes or conditions of our mind: the doing mode and the being mode. The doing mode is activated when your mind wishes to rectify a discrepancy. The being mode is directed at acknowledging what there is now. Mindfulness training teaches you to switch between the two.

Incidentally, in both cases it is not only about a mental reaction but also a physical one. The whole body (muscles, hormones, nerves, brains) is activated in an appropriate way.

16 Daniel Goleman, Richard Boyatzis, and Annie McKee, *Primal Leadership. Realizing the Power of Emotional Intelligence* (Boston: Harvard Business School Press, 2002). 6.

17 1Rients Ritskes, *Leer denken wat je wil denken* (Rotterdam: Asoka, 2010).

Doing mode

The doing mode is the mode for addressing things and changing them. What is happening now does not match the expectation of how you would have liked it or how it should be. Our whole body-mind system is made ready for action. Mindfulness trainer, Rob Brandsma, writes: You walk to get from A to B, you wash your hands to clean them, you eat to ease your hunger. Doing has given us inventions and taken us to the moon. The whole economy depends on doing. Doing mode is an instrument for the future. That is fine: in that way you get around something."[18]

The effect of detecting a discrepancy is that old patterns of habit are immediately activated to close the gap and to allow the associated negative feelings to flow away. Once that has happened, you can exit doing mode again. A glass of water falls over, and you run to the kitchen to get a mop. Wipe it up. Done. Until the mind, and that is generally very fast, discovers a new discrepancy.

But what if it is not immediately apparent what must be done? Take the example of an employee who has considerable expertise, but is not very handy in social interaction with colleagues: he is blunt and barks at others. As his manager, you're torn between the feeling that you can't do without him and finding his behavior unacceptable. You've tried everything, nothing seems to help. And perhaps you begin to doubt your own capacity as a leader. The discrepancy persists. The result is that your mind keeps on processing all information in doing mode, keeps on churning things over. Sometimes it may disappear into the background if more urgent matters have to be addressed. But ultimately the unsolved question surfaces again once the urgency of the other task has decreased.

Doing mode feels like a recurring, unsatisfying feeling. That is because our mind is constantly checking and reviewing whether the detected discrepancy has been solved. Whether the gap has grown smaller. An ingrained characteristic of our mind. If things occur about which nothing can be done immediately, all that re-

18 Rob Brandsma, *Beter nu* (Den Haag: Scriptum, 2007). 42.

mains is for our mind to keep manipulating its ideas, its proposals for what should happen in the hope and expectation that there is nevertheless a way of narrowing the gap. We know all about that in organizations. How often do dissatisfied employees firmly hold onto the hope that tomorrow, or next week, or with a new manager, things will be better?

A powerful side effect of this functioning of our mind is that those thoughts, ideas, and suggestions acquire an increasingly "real" character. Through a repetition of thoughts, patterns arise which are assumed to be true. Current experiences, for example the kind words from a colleague who is normally rather nasty, simply go unnoticed. Analyzing the future and the past has such a high priority that the here and now has disappeared into the background. There is only success or failure, all or nothing.

Being mode

The counterpart to doing mode is being mode. Being mode is focused on allowing and acknowledging what there is without any pressure to change anything. When our attention allows those experiences, it is not concerned with ascertaining discrepancies and then taking action to reduce them. The effect is that relaxation, space, openness arises.

> *"You can't do being. You don't have to achieve anything with being. Being is simply there. You don't have to go anywhere. You don't have to achieve anything. Perhaps you remember when you were still a child and played with building bricks or dressed your doll: the [process of] building and dressing was the most enjoyable. [...]. The aim of playing is playing itself."*[19]

Where do the differences between doing and being come from? First of all, being mode does not have the aim of combating discrepancy. Another difference is the way doing and being deal with time. The purposeful character of the doing mode means that you are constantly trying to estimate the consequences of the actions

19 Ibid., 42-43.

you carry out. In your thoughts, you anticipate the situation when your aim has been achieved, estimate how long it will take and what the possible dangers are that could prevent you from achieving your aim. Or you take a good look at what you can learn from the past in order to reach your aim as quickly and successfully as possible. In short, your mind is constantly wandering forward into the future or backward into the past. You are only occasionally in the here and now.

That is different in being mode. You don't have to do anything, don't have to go anywhere. And so you can concentrate fully on the experiences of the moment, completely direct your attention on what there is now. In being mode, you can experience most immediately and deeply what there is now.

Another difference between doing and being is how thoughts and feelings are dealt with. For setting and achieving aims, our mind places great import on conceptual thinking. Concepts are seen as a reflection or interpretation of reality and form the basis for action in the doing mode. Feelings are immediately interpreted as either "good" or "bad." And our mind is out to allow the good feelings to persist and to get rid of the bad ones as quickly as possible. In this way, certainly in our culture of emotions, feelings acquire the status of things to which you must aspire. "You must feel good!" becomes an imperative.

In being mode, thoughts and feelings do not really have any status different from all the other aspects of the experience of the moment. Feelings and thoughts are events, just like sounds or physical stimuli, which surface in our mind, receive attention, and then pass on. They are thus detached from the pressure for targeted action. And so thoughts and feelings, even if they are familiar patterns, do not trigger an automatic reaction. The effect is a greater tolerance for discomfort, but without a specific reaction to that discomfort. Even thoughts such as "now do this, now do that" do not lead to a reflex reaction, but you learn to see them as events in the mind. That creates space for a conscious reaction.

A final difference is that space arises in being mode for a feeling of freshness, openness to new experiences or aspects thereof. Space for complexity and versatility in the moment. While in doing

Doing mode	Being mode
Action	Rest
Effort	Relaxation
Future-oriented	Directed at the here and now
Achieve, reach, overcome	Process, regenerate, learn
Activating hormones	Connecting hormones
Sympathetic nervous system	Parasympathetic nervous system
Left cerebral hemisphere	Right cerebral hemisphere
Attention directed at mental information	Attention open to all fields of experience
Attention with targeted focus	Attention with playful, limited focus
Thoughts are persistent, directing	Thoughts are loose and associative
Routine	Unique response, experiment, tentative
Energy toward the outside, extremities	Energy to the centre, stomach
Functional attitude toward the other	Open, approaching attitude toward the other
Feeling of being isolated from the world	Feeling of being connected with the world

mode, it is exactly that diversity of dimensions that is reduced to one overruling dimension: in this concept, precisely this action is the solution, and no other. For that is the way to achieve your aim.[20]

Allow me here to clear away a misunderstanding: being mode does not imply doing nothing or passivity. Nothing is further from the truth. The example of children who become absorbed in playing contradicts this; there is creativity and pleasure in their play. And so you can be very active in being mode. But you are not exclusively and constantly focused on the result. There is confidence

20 Segal, Williams, and Teasdale, *Aandachtgerichte cognitieve therapie bij depressie*: 66-68.

that you will arrive at that result, even when you are acting from moment to moment. With attention for the action itself. It looks like the flow of the action, or like the moment that a golfer experiences just before he releases his downswing, as described so beautifully by Gallwey in his classic *The Inner Game of Golf.*[21]

Brandsma gives a fine summary of the two conditions of our body-mind system in his thoughtful *Mindfulness Basis Book.*[22]

Doing and being in organizations

In organizations, you can distinguish two mindsets, comparable to the doing mode and the being mode at an individual level. One mindset is fixed, risk-avoiding and limiting, sharply focused on how it should be and directed at enforcing that. The other is open, inquiring and more directed at what is going to come. In the culture of an organization with a fixed mindset, the doing mode is central, with all the risks involved, and in the second one, a better balance is struck between doing and being, with greater space for innovation.

Fixed mindset	Open mindset
Doing without overview	Knowing what you are doing
Action takes priority over reflection	Regularly switching between action and reflection
Suppress disagreeable information	Open for deviating information
Vertical decision-making	Horizontal dialogue
Winning or losing	Win-win
Focused only on results	Focused on results and collaboration
Settling scores with each other	Learning from each other

21 Timothy Gallwey, *The Inner Game of Golf* (New York: Random House, 2009).

22 Rob Brandsma, *Mindfulness basisboek. Kennis, achtergrond en toepassing* (Houten: LannooCampus, 2012). 62. The table has been adjusted for linguistic purposes.

Two examples will clarify the difference between the behavior in the organization of a manager with a fixed mindset and one with an open mindset. The first is Johan, manager at a telecom provider:

> *"I discovered that we had a rather rigid world view and operated from it. That caused a fierce discussion at work. When the marketing department published new data about disappointing sales, I got angry. And I ordered my people in the sales team to ratchet it up a notch with the same approach. Without thinking about it. I immediately stamped out any objections from my team members, because I knew my boss was expecting me to hit my targets next month. I was negative about the motives of my colleagues who commented on things, and this meant that I interpreted the situation from that perspective. If I had been more inquisitive, I could have asked what had caused their reaction, but I knew better. And the result was that we got into a fight."*

The more open mindset is illustrated by the example of Suzanne, who is a partner at a large law firm:

> *"In our work, winning or losing is naturally very important. But we always consciously choose to work toward a win-win situation. When we start working with clients, we consciously adopt a more investigative attitude. Even if clients are mainly interested in getting their own back on the other party. With frustrated and defensive clients, we practice exploring all options and only then drawing up a strategy. For this we work in teams in order to have as diverse a range of knowledge as possible and to learn from each other."*

These examples show how the fixed mindset in an organization's culture leads to setting the possibilities in stone, while an open mindset leads to new perspectives. And how, because of this, mutual communication between people is directed.

Attentiveness: recognize every experience

Now that we have an idea of what mindfulness is and we have seen what switching between doing and being looks like, it is time to ask ourselves how we can develop mindfulness. You do that by paying conscious attention to the experiences that present themselves from moment to moment. You train your attentiveness. It is about taking note of your experiences, whether they come from the outside or from the inside. Just like the reflex reactions to those experiences, which are often aimed at holding on to them or pushing them away. And at the same time you train yourself to respond to those experiences and the associated reflex reactions with an attitude of curiosity and mildness or compassion toward yourself.[23]

Let me use an example to illustrate how developing the ability for mindfulness works in both aspects, increasing the attentiveness and strengthening the supporting attitude.

I offer this example based on an experience during one of my first mindfulness retreats. I had registered for it as part of my education as a mindfulness trainer, and I didn't really know what to expect. I had worked hard right up to the start of the retreat, and I arrived with a lot of unresolved matters that I found difficult to put aside. Meditating proved difficult; my head was spinning with thoughts about all those difficult matters. And what's more, after just one day, every bit of my body hurt. My feet and legs hurt, I had difficulty sitting up straight and I constantly yearned for the day to end and to take a long sleep. I didn't succeed in calming everything down by feeling my breathing. My attention constantly bounced away from me like a tennis ball. And the pain seized me every time I tried to relax. Meditation became almost unbearable, it made me crazy, angry, frustrated. Why couldn't it be easier, and why did I have to feel all that pain? Was there any point in meditating?

When I explained my condition to the teacher, he reacted kindly. He recognized my pain and explained that it wasn't unusual to experience this in the beginning. He asked me to close my eyes and

23 J. Mark G. Williams, "Mindfulness, Depression and Modes of Mind," *Cognitive Therapy Research* 32 (2008): 721-33.

take note of the condition of my body, which was filled with ten-
sion. With his help, I was able to accept the tension somewhat and
suffer it with a little more kind attention. I breathed, relaxed a lit-
tle and understood that what I needed was nothing other than to
recognize my own pain. I was forcing myself not to feel any pain
and so I was constantly in a fight with myself. With the instruction
to keep that kind attention for my body, I returned to the medita-
tion room. The following day I was able to notice that my body
cramped up and my anger grew. But I was also able to accept that
and with this, a first relaxation arose in my body. Slowly the in-
sight grew that my body was a sort of mirror and that my kind at-
tentiveness showed me both the cause of and the remedy for my
discomfort, by recognizing the tension in my mind and consciously
relaxing that tension.
As the days progressed, my insight became more and more precise.
I noticed that my anger and anxiety about everything that I still
had to do as a management consultant had brought about these
tensions in my body. Trying to keep everything under control, but
that had clearly failed. I was here, and could do nothing about the
unresolved issues. And so, as the end of the retreat came nearer, the
relaxation grew and I also saw the advantage of curiosity about
and openness toward my own discomfort and painful experiences.

What this example shows is that the growth of my attentiveness
didn't automatically lead to relaxation; quite the opposite, I would
almost say. But with the growth of attentiveness and kindness for
my own experiences, the attitudinal qualities that are associated
with mindfulness also developed: curiosity and openness. It is all
about having the courage to observe everything without any reservation. I call this, in common with the American meditation
teacher, Jack Kornfield, *fearless presence.*[24] By having the courage
to take stock of all experiences, a freer attitude arises that allows an
easier way of distancing yourself from the autopilot and learning
to switch between doing and being.

24 Jack Kornfield, *The Wise Heart* (London: Rider, 2008). 95. Kornfield
   calls this "fearless presence" an act of courage.

This reversal in our attitude is the core of the transformation process that you undergo in mindfulness training. That process of the training of attentiveness has four components:[25]

> **Transformation of experience through attentiveness**
> • Recognition
> • Acceptance
> • Investigation
> • Non-identification

Recognition

Recognition, or allowing what is based on a willingness to face something. We do not react to awkward experiences or information with the attitude of "nothing wrong" but with the attitude of "let's take a moment and see what it is." We no longer suppress painful experiences, but try to view them from a certain distance. We no longer close ourselves off, do not roughly suppress the experience or information, but allow it to enter our consciousness. We recognize and see that an experience is asking for attention.

It is the first step toward freeing ourselves from an ingrained mental picture or operating according to a fixed routine and the autopilot. And with that recognition, we move away from denial or avoiding what is to be seen. The leader who has fallen into the trap of stress and sacrifice, looks at himself in the mirror. He is much more aware of the first signals. The team dares to accept that new information contradicts the proposed way of working and has the courage to stop fixed routines and decision procedures. The company realizes that the production process causes serious environmental damage and that it is part of a larger system and enters into a green alliance, as Coca-Cola did.

25 Ibid., 101-05. This process is known under the acronym. RAIN (recognition, acceptance, investigation, non-identification).

Acceptance

The next component is the development of an attitude of acceptance of the facts as they are. Leaving data for what they are also helps defuse the sometimes subtle resistance that accompanies the acceptance of the reality of experiences or information. How often do we discover in ourselves a desire for something to be slightly different or prove to be different when we observe something awkward. Acceptance means an attitude in which the experience is allowed to its full extent, whether it is pleasant or not. We release our reticence and adopt an attitude of: "things are as they are, whether I understand them or can place them or not." That enables us to make our tense relationship with the experience somewhat more relaxed.

A word of warning is appropriate here about the use of the word "acceptance." We are easily inclined to think that acceptance means the same as no possibility of change. The opposite is true; it is actually a courageous step: "Trouble? Life is trouble. Only death is nice. Life is rolling up your sleeves and embracing trouble," in the words of Zorba the Greek.[26]

With acceptance, a problem often shifts from unsolvable to more or less manageable, and that is a big step forward. Many parents have to deal with their children refusing to eat certain foods. Children resist and parents persist. Until a day arrives when the parents give up the struggle and no longer try to force something on their children. And a miracle occurs. The children decide to try the food after all. Apparently the resistance was not so much directed at the food but at the parents' insistence. By accepting the resistance and leaving it for what it is, a manageable openness often arises.

Acceptance is also of great importance for leadership and organizations. But acceptance is not the usual attitude among leaders or managers, and here mindfulness seems to collide with the determination of leadership and management to lead and manage. But the importance of acceptance appears pregnant at moments of crisis in organizations. In a situation, for example, that requires the immediate recall of products – think of the contamination of Per-

26 Ibid., 102.

rier bottles with polluted spring water a few years ago – the first advice managers receive from crisis communication experts is: don't defend yourself, accept the situation for what it is (even if you disagree with it).

Acceptance, acknowledging matters, could very well prove a good correction to that attitude that is frequently so prevalent in the leadership of companies to "simply fix" any problems that may arise. And therefore underestimating the possibilities for self-understanding and self-correction and of the learning ability of organizations and people. Work is then based on (enforced) strength instead of mobilizing the energy present for change. Let me stress that this is no plea for endless friendliness. For friendliness without clear awareness is not very handy. And sugar-coating unpleasant matters can easily lead to defensive avoidance.

Like acceptance, "compassion" is not a term with much credence in the world of organizations. And yet Ed Schein, the grandmaster of cultural change and leadership in organizations, explicitly points out that the capacity of leaders to bear *together with the employees* the discomfort of organizations is an important factor for success in change processes.[27]

We know from the therapeutic relationship that self-acceptance and self-compassion, the relationship we have with ourselves, is important for how we observe the reality around us and for an effective process with clients. That effectiveness can be advanced by exercising mindfulness. The same applies to leaders of organizations. Mindfulness helps you to be open to different perspectives,[28] recognize the emotional reality, and avoid a blinkered focus.[29] And that his behavior and attitude is appropriate for leadership that directs the attention at what the situation demands.

27 Edgar H. Schein, *Organizational Culture and Leadership* (San Francisco: Jossey Bass, 2010). 381.
28 Langer, *Mindfulness.*
29 Richard Boyatzis and Annie McKee, *Resonant Leadership* (Cambridge: Harvard Business Press, 2005). 124.

Investigation

The more complete investigation of the reality is the third component of attentiveness and this is facilitated by recognizing our dilemmas and accepting what there is without any reticence. We now ask ourselves the question of what exactly is happening and take a deeper look at the nature of our experiences.[30] In doing this, we look at our bodily sensations, such as tension, warmth or cold, hardness, and the associated tone of our feelings: pleasant, unpleasant, or neutral. We may discover patterns and recognize them and our reactions to them from other situations. We also look at our thoughts, images, associations, and emotions. The stories that we tell ourselves in our mind about the situation or experience. And then perhaps discover habit patterns or obsolete mental images. And we look at a broader elaboration of concepts, connected in life and the world, and the degree to which we cling on to them. This latter is, in particular, a broad area, where we look at the development of patterns of experience, the composition – if we look at things at an organizational level – of the culture, the question of how we relate to this: can we direct it or is it a pattern that apparently has a life of its own? Are we stuck with it, do we rise up against it or can we leave it for what it is? Is it productive and does it makes us rigid?

Non-identification

Finally, we arrive at the last component of the process of attentiveness: letting go of the identification with the experience. With this we mean that we stop identifying ourselves with the experience, we no longer limit ourselves through a fixed interpretation of that experience. We look at things openly and freely and may be able to attach a new significance to the experience. We create space for ourselves to be different than we thought, or to act differently. Let-

30 The Buddhist tradition offers us four fields of research: the body, our feelings, the world of thought, and that of the dharma, the area of the elements and the patterns from which reality is composed. See: Kornfield, *The Wise Heart*: 103-04.

ting go of the identification with a behavior pattern from the auto-pilot or the fixed mindset of an organizational culture releases us from the dependency on not doing or wanting anything else. It overcomes the inclination to oppose change by organizing immunity. And it thus releases us from the tension of steeling ourselves against anything new or to putting energy into retaining what already exists, from the constant anxieties about it that are always present in the background.

Getting to it mindfully: insight and connection

With the four components dealt with above, we nurture a greater attentiveness, the core of mindfulness. But there is another side to mindfulness training which cannot be seen as separate from it. In addition to attentiveness and focus, the uninhibited observation of bodily sensations and their appreciation, sounds, thoughts and emotions, it is also about nurturing a supportive attitude, of mildness to yourself and solidarity with others. If you want to observe without inhibition, you must develop an attitude in which all experiences, whether pleasant or not, uncomfortable or painful, are welcome. A non-judgmental attitude too: judgment can be suspended or set aside. The Belgian psychiatrist and Zen Buddhist, Edel Maex, describes this as two sides of the same coin. One side represents the cognitive element, the attentiveness and the other ethical element, the attitude of acceptance of how it is for now and the experience of solidarity with the whole. He sees them as inseparable, like the flame and the heat, the one is a function of the other. Feeling connected to or responsible for naturally arises from the development of understanding. Without solidarity with the whole, no understanding is possible.[31]

Jon Kabat-Zinn has described that attitude in mindfulness training in seven qualities. These attitudes help define the way in which attentiveness is deployed. Experiences are viewed from a certain attitude, not just like that: the core of that attitude is that the expe-

---

31 Edel Maex, "The Buddhist Roots of Mindfulnesstraining: A Practitioners View," *Contemporary Buddhism* 12, no. 11 (2011).

rience is okay as it is. Brandsma shows how they work as an antidote to the autopilot in ourselves.[32] In the table below, we list in the
first column the attitude that supports the development of attentiveness and mindfulness. But if you reverse those attitudes and
strengthen them with additional thoughts, as indicated in the second and third columns, you can see how attitudes of not okay (toward the experience) trigger the autopilot and even evoke our fear
of change as the mind bolts (column three).

Experience is okay: attitude	Experience is not okay: attitude	Experience is not okay: thought
Acceptance	Rejection	Not this!
Don't judge	Judge	Good! Not good!
Trust	Distrust	What to do now?
Patience	Impatience	It must change!
Don't endeavor	Endeavor	Do something!
Don't know ('beginner's mind')	Know (familiar framework)	Already know it!
Let go	Hold on	Persist!

By training attentiveness and the associated attitudes from the
first column, you make it possible for yourself to stop the autopilot and to address the underlying immune reaction to change.

By learning to switch mentally between doing and being through
the transformation process of attentiveness, you develop the basis
for mindful leadership. You learn to work with your attention,
with that of yourself and that of your organization. Now that we
have seen what mindfulness is and how you learn, by switching
between doing and being, to start working with attention, it is now
time, in the next chapter, to see how you can learn the basic skills
of mindful management yourself.

---

32 Brandsma, *Mindfulness basisboek. Kennis, achtergrond en toepassing*: 61.

References

Bishop, S., M. Lau, S. Shapiro, L. Carlson, N. Anderson, and J. Carmody. "Mindfulness: A Proposed Operational Definition." *Clinical Psychology: Science and Practice* 11, no. 3 (2004): 230-41.

Boyatzis, Richard, and Annie McKee. *Resonant Leadership*. Cambridge: Harvard Business Press, 2005.

Brandsma, Rob. *Beter nu*. Den Haag: Scriptum, 2007.

————. *Mindfulness basisboek. Kennis, achtergrond en toepassing*. Houten: LannooCampus, 2012.

Epstein, Mark. *Gedachten zonder denker. Psychotherapie vanuit boeddhistisch perspectief*. Rotterdam: Asoka, 2007.

Gallwey, Timothy. *The Inner Game of Golf*. New York: Random House, 2009.

Goleman, Daniel, Richard Boyatzis, and Annie McKee. *Primal Leadership. Realizing the Power Emotional Intelligence*. Boston: Harvard Business School Press, 2002.

Kabat-Zinn, Jon. *Coming to Our Senses*. New York: Hyperion, 2005.

————. *Handboek meditatief ontspannen*. Haarlem: Altamira-Becht, 2004.

————. *Waar je ook gaat, daar ben je*. Utrecht: Servire, 2006.

Kornfield, Jack. *The Wise Heart*. London: Rider, 2008.

Koster, Frits. *Bevrijdend inzicht*. Rotterdam: Asoka, 1999.

Langer, Ellen. *Mindfulness*. Cambridge: Perseus, 1989.

Maex, Edel. "The Buddhist Roots of Mindfulnesstraining: A Practitioners View." *Contemporary Buddhism* 12, no. 11 (2011): 165-75.

Ritskes, Rients. *Leer denken wat je wil denken*. Rotterdam: Asoka, 2010.

Schein, Edgar H. *Organizational Culture and Leadership*. San Francisco: Jossey Bass, 2010.

Segal, Zindel V., J. Mark G. Williams, and John D. Teasdale. *Aandachtgerichte cognitieve therapie bij depressie*. Amsterdam: Uitgeverij Nieuwezijds, 2006.

Siegel, J. Daniel. *Mindsight. The New Science of Personal Transformation*. New York: Bantam Books, 2010.

Weick, Karl E., and Kathleen M. Sutcliffe. *Managing the Unexpected*. San Francisco: John Wiley & Sons, 2010.

Williams, J. Mark G. "Mindfulness, Depression and Modes of Mind." *Cognitive Therapy Research* 32 (2008): 721-33.

Williams, J. Mark G., and Jon Kabat-Zinn. "Mindfulness: Diverse Perspectives on Its Meaning, Origins, and Multiple Applications at the Intersection of Science and Dharma." *Contemporary Buddhism* 12, no. 1 (2011): 1-18.

3
Building your core: resilience and an open mind

"We are always practicing. In other words, the body is incapable of not practicing. And what we practice we become"[1].

Richard Strozzi-Heckler – leadership trainer

In the previous chapter we learned about doing and being as two positions in our body-mind system. Doing is our everyday position. And to be able to switch, we must learn being. That is what mindfulness training is about. And so training mindfulness starts with a paradox, for if you are to learn to be, you must do something – namely, train.

In order to switch mentally, you need resilience, and in this chapter I will show you how you can increase the space for a conscious response when dealing with stressful experiences.

Before I discuss the components for the basic mindfulness training for managers, I will first deal briefly with the core difference in attention in the doing mode and the being mode. Also, I will deal with the qualities of managers in handling experiences and stress. Qualities that can easily turn into pitfalls.

In the main part of this chapter I shall present all the basic exercises in mindfulness training for managers.

---

1 Quoted in Doug Silsbee, *The Mindful Coach* (San Francisco: Jossey-Bass, 2010). 201.

Resilience: learning the game of switching

If you are to lay the foundation for your mindful leadership, you will have to learn the game of switching between doing mode and being mode, the core of mindful self-management. Both modes deal with attention in very different ways. In doing mode, our attention is focused, directed at the task. And when things are less tense, attention wanes. It is also difficult to release that focus. If you've been working intensively on something for a while, you feel that focus echo mentally and physically for a while after the moment that you have let it go. In being mode, our attention is spread and not focused. Everything and anything can come in. It is agile, less judgmental, you could almost say free and easy. Brandsma places the qualities of attention in both modes next to each other:[2]

Attention in doing mode	Attention in being mode
Autopilot	Conscious response
Either focused or distracted	Broadly present
Directed, strong focus	Playful, light focus
Identifying (be consumed)	Lightly touching ('dancing')
Divisive	Integral
Directed at mental information	Open for all sources of experience

Developing the ability for mindfulness makes it possible to adjust how you dose your attention to what the situation demands: focused in doing mode and relaxed in being mode. The following exercises help to master this method of working with attention. You develop resilience, learn to stop doing, and make use of being, to see clearly and to maintain balance.

Based on the experiences with our mindfulness training programs for managers, my colleague, Rob Brandsma, and I have identified

2 Rob Brandsma, *Mindfulness basisboek. Kennis, achtergrond en toepassing* (Houten: LannooCampus, 2012). 76.

a number of pitfalls into which managers can fall when withstanding stress:[3]

- Managers have developed an enormous ability to withstand stress, but that does not mean they are capable of coping with stress in an effective manner. The result is that they have difficulty in maintaining a proper balance between work and personal life and often take insufficient time for physical and mental recovery.
- Managers are great at framing experiences and associated problems in a suitable context. They can rapidly identify something conceptually and then "pigeonhole" it. In this way, the problem is stated, but whether this also leads to getting rid of the experience remains to be seen.
- Managers are good at taking concrete measures. An awkward issue is quickly disposed of in a procedural agreement. A matter is delegated or quickly pushed on to somebody else. Sometimes that works well, but at other times it flies back like a boomerang.
- Managers regularly interpret their functional responsibility as their purely personal responsibility. It is certainly motivational, but at the same time it can easily lead to a lack of clarity in demarcating responsibilities and to the idea that a manager must be available 24/7.
- Managers sometimes also tip the balance in the opposite direction, but then not toward themselves but toward their employees. Then functional responsibility reigns and is implemented with such emphasis on business that there is little room for the emotional side of leadership.

Managers have a trenchant skill for dealing well with stress and are good at stating solutions and organizing action. These qualities are strengths in a manager, but, if they are deployed too frequently and too automatically, they can become pitfalls. Mindfulness allows you to see these patterns and detaches them, as it were, so that you can adequately deploy these qualities but, if necessary, choose alternate options. Using mindfulness training, you can learn not to endure stress any longer and take it all on your shoulders, but to

3 Ibid., 180.

handle it more effectively and thus, as manager, develop a greater space for a conscious response.

Because managers can take quite a bit and therefore easily fall into the pitfall of self-sacrifice and of taking and continuing to take responsibility, we concentrate first on building resilience in the training of managers, on our ability to recover from the difficulty, the pressure and the adversities of life, whether small or large, many or few. Some have a greater capacity for this than others. What one person sees as an interesting challenge can be an insurmountable mountain for another. Psychology has taught us that resilience goes hand in hand with various psychological traits: the feeling of control, commitment, and challenge. It has also been established that some people can deal better with external stress because a situation makes inherent sense to them and they can concentrate on the fact that they can direct life and that they can understand their situation. They can, in principle, fathom it, even though, at first glance, it may seem unmanageable and confusing. The research that Jon Kabat-Zinn did into his classic mindfulness-based stress reduction (MBSR) training indicated that people who took the training developed greater toughness and resilience.[4]

Training mindfulness is learning to be with all experiences that present themselves to you in the moment, as we saw in the previous chapter. You observe them and, no matter what the nature of these experiences is – sometimes they are pleasant, sometimes neutral, and sometimes simply awkward or extremely annoying – you do not run away from them, do not try to brush them aside, nor do you make any attempt to change them. For the moment, you just accept them for what they are. Dealing with experiences in this way is completely different to how we usually handle them, especially the awkward ones. By trying to internalize them – actually, a form of storing them away – or interpreting them so that they appear less awkward and the associated feeling becomes softer and less intrusive. Or when pleasant, trying to prolong such experiences. This is not how you work when training mindfulness.

4   Mark Williams and Danny Penman, *Mindfulness* (Amsterdam: Nieuwezijds, 2011). 64-65.

You work on experiencing both awkward and pleasant feelings as they are and accepting them without holding on to them.

Mindfulness training – sometimes we call it also resilience training – makes you aware of a number of new fields of attention, which together form the active constituents. Below, I shall describe the following aspects of the training:

- The wealth of seven senses
- Insight into the autopilot
- Signals from the body
- Handling stress: stretching without striving
- The art of pausing
- The limits of your availability
- Active sensing instead of feeling good
- Differentiating between your thoughts and yourself

For each of these fields of attention, I will describe exercises which you can use to expose, explore, and practice the theme.

The richness of seven senses

The first step in virtually every mindfulness training is to become aware of the enormous wealth of experiences that arise through our senses. We detect images, sounds, smells, and tastes and we can feel a touch on the skin, warmth/cold and pain and pleasure. Furthermore, we can observe the balancing of our body, a process that generally happens subconsciously, and we can, from within, discern our body or parts of our body. We do this with our familiar five senses: sight, hearing, smell, taste, touch. Some add our sixth sense to this: our own observation of our body or proprioception.[5] In common terms, this is also referred to as our intuition. And psychiatrist Daniel Siegel calls our ability to look inside and observe our mind as our seventh sense, *mindsight*.[6] We are talking then about our conscious observation, our attentiveness.

5   Jon Kabat-Zinn, *Coming to Our Senses* (New York: Hyperion, 2005). 217-19.
6   J. Daniel Siegel, *Mindsight. The New Science of Personal Transformation* (New York: Bantam Books, 2010). xiii.

Below I describe the raisin exercise that is used in almost every mindfulness training to discover what happens when you open your mind to a whole range of experiences from your seven senses.

Raisin exercise: all senses

Take five to ten minutes, during which you can sit on your own in a quiet place. Make sure you are not disturbed; turn off your cell phone. You need a few raisins or some other dried fruit. Your assignment is to eat these raisins or fruits in a mindful way, using the following instructions. Take 20 to 30 seconds for each step.

1. Hold

Take one of the raisins or pieces of dried fruit and hold it in the palm of your hand or between your thumb and forefinger. Concentrate on it and approach it as if it were something you had never seen before in your life. Do you feel its weight on your hand? Does it cast a shadow across your palm?

2. Look

Take the time to really look at the raisin. Imagine that you have never seen one before. Look at it extremely carefully and with full attention. Let your eyes examine every single part of it. Study the places where it catches the light, the dark dips, the creases and wrinkles.

3. Touch

Turn the raisin around between your fingers and test how the surface feels. How does it feel between the thumb and index finger of the other hand? Notice the movements in your muscles and joints as you are doing this. Slightly press the raisin and notice how that gives you a feeling of its inner texture.

4. Smell

Now slowly raise the raisin, with full attention for the movement of your hands and fingers, to your nose and determine what you observe with each intake of breath. Does it have an odor? Let it fill your awareness. If it has little or no odor, notice that as well. Observe any changes that may take place in your mouth or stomach, such as salivating.

5. Place

Take the raisin to your lips and study the delicate sensation of touch here. Then place it in your mouth but do not start chewing. Let the raisin rest for a moment on your tongue and observe what happens. Let it move over your tongue and bring it into contact with the roof of your mouth. Note what happens in your body.

6. Taste

Now take the first bite. Exactly one and no more. Ascertain which taste or tastes are released. Then take another bite. What changes then in the taste? Continue chewing on the raisin bite for bite, but without swallowing. Continue until there is no longer any perceptible shape or form left.

7. Swallow

Form the intention to swallow the raisin or what is left of it. Notice your intention before you actually swallow. Observe what your tongue does in preparation for the actual swallowing. Can you also follow the sensations of swallowing, from the rear of your mouth to your throat and into your stomach?

8. After effects

Pause to consider all the stages of the exercise and the effects it has generated. Do you still taste an after taste? Did thoughts arise as you were doing it? Would you almost automatically pick up another raisin and eat it?

Take the time to note all your experiences and thoughts.

To participants in our trainings, this exercise is often surprising, no matter how familiar the raisin is. Surprising because, for example, there are so many different experiences that can be derived from one small raisin. Or because suddenly the smell of a raisin is so new. Or because somebody notices how we are used to swallowing a raisin on autopilot. Something else which may come as a new experience is the whole series of preparatory actions that the body undertakes at the moment we bring the raisin to the mouth. Salivary glands, tongue, breathing, lips: everything is brought into use. And how often does it take a lot of effort to prevent the reflex of swallowing the raisin before you have chewed it really fine.

"I never realized how much smell a raisin has. And, by the way, I didn't like the smell one little bit. Caused a bit of aversion in me, which only went away when I had taken it in my mouth."

"I had swallowed it before I was aware of it. It happened all by itself."

"A raisin is really sickly sweet. I'm completely full after eating just one of them."

"I have to work really hard to do the exercise step by step. My body always wanted to rush ahead of where we were. Gee, it takes a lot of effort to do it with attentiveness!"

"What on earth has this got to do with management? If the people at work could see me now..."

The simple raisin exercise teaches us various things. To start with, the wealth of experience we can derive from eating just one small piece of dried fruit. All that we have to do for that is not simply pop it in our mouth and swallow, but to do everything step by step and with attention and we have our fill of experiences. Experiences which also generate thoughts and judgments and that gives you an image of your mental reactions to the experiences: the smell you don't like, or imagining your colleagues back at work seeing you do this. And what we notice is that we are so full of these types of automatic reactions that our body is already in the doing mode of eating and swallowing, while in the exercise we have only reached the point of bringing the raisin to our lips.

Above all, the exercise shows how many signals and experiences you miss in your daily life, how many you ignore or perhaps suppress. And so the raisin exercise is a first training in the basic skill of mindfulness: noticing things, from moment to moment.

Insight into the autopilot

A second theme, next to that of observing the sensual experiences, is becoming aware of the autopilot in our work and daily life. It starts by getting an idea of your automatic reactions during the raisin exercise. But you can extend this by paying attention to how you carry out all sorts of activities throughout the day. There are also a number of suitable exercises for this. The core of this type of exercise is to carry out routine daily actions with attention. That can, for example, be the way you come into the office in the morning and switch on your computer. Or the way in which – probably without much thought – you drink your first cup of coffee. Or how, at home, you carry out an everyday action such as brushing your teeth.

Doing a routine action with attention

Resolve in the coming week to do one routine action each day with attention. Choose for this a simple action which you generally do in the same way. You don't need to do the action differently than normal. You do not need to enjoy it more or do it in a special way. The assignment is simply to do the action with your complete attention and then to observe what you experience.

Examples:
- The first cup of coffee at work
- Switching on the computer at the start of the day
- Brushing your teeth
- Placing the trash in the container
- Etcetera...

See whether you can do the exercise each time as an experiment, with eyes and ears wide open, as if it were completely new to you.

It is apparently not that easy to do routine actions with attention. You quickly notice that you do them mind*less*ly and forget to pause. The autopilot takes over. And if you do succeed, then the routine action with attention often confronts you with the flurry in your head. As you take your first sips of coffee, all sorts of thoughts about the things you have to do today or the things you had left undone yesterday run through your head.

In order to train mindfulness, you must first begin by learning to pay attention, to make your attention more focused. And you must be capable of recognizing and breaking through habit patterns. This is dealt with in the following exercises.

Signals from the body

One of the core principles of exercising mindfulness is realizing the importance of the body and using physical signals. That is not taken for granted in our Western culture. We live in a culture in which, since Descartes, the body has become rather undervalued. *Cogito ergo sum* has gained the upper hand. Although it is, in itself, a nice simplification of our body-mind system, it has been raised to an absolute contradiction and thus misses insight into the constant interaction and feedback between body and mind. As Westerners, we do not learn to make good use of signals from our body. And yet research shows that those signals still influence us, even if we block the physical sensations from our consciousness. The neural input from the body and the emotions unconsciously influences our reasoning and decision-making.[7]

An interesting experiment was held in the early 1980s. Students were asked to assess the quality of headphones. They had to listen to music and a speech and rate the quality of the sound. During the listening session, one group was asked to nod yes with their head, the other group to shake no. The third group had to keep their heads still. The highest score for quality of the headphones was given by the group that was asked to nod yes. Even more interesting was the result of a follow-up experiment in which the students participated (without their knowledge) as they left. Here questions were posed about student life and the level of college tuition, whether the latter should be raised from 587 dollars to 750 dollars and what a good level for college tuition would be. Those who had to keep their heads still mentioned an average around the current amount. Those who had shaken no gave a lower average, and those who had nodded yes felt – honestly! – that college tuition should be raised considerably. What the experiment taught us is that the judgment we make from moment to moment is influenced by the condition of our body at the moment of judging.[8] And that shows how important it can be to make full use of the signals from our body. Certainly, in management positions, this is an underesti-

7   Ibid., 125.
8   Williams and Penman, *Mindfulness*: 104-05.

mated force. There is, therefore, every reason to learn that capacity better. In mindfulness training, various exercises are used for this. One exercise is an attentive exploration of the body and the signals it broadcasts. The other consists of moving attentively, either standing or seated, through a series of yoga exercises.

Body scan

Begin by laying full stretch on a mat or cushion. Make yourself comfortable. You can lie on the floor or on your bed and you should do it in a place that is warm and where you will not be disturbed.

Gently close your eyes, observe the movement of your breathing and become aware of the physical sensations in your body. The first will probably be the contact points your body has with the mat or the cushion. Take the time to adjust to this position and let yourself sink deeper in the mat or bed with each breath.

Make yourself aware in a friendly way that this is a moment of "falling awake." Falling asleep is for another time. The aim of the exercise is not to relax or calm down, even though this could very well be the effect. The intention is to observe all sensations that occur from moment to moment in your body when you systematically explore the body from head to toe. Sometimes you will feel nothing, and that, too, is fine. If you do not observe any sensations, you do not need to imagine them. Try to do this with an open and curious attitude.

Incidentally, it can be that the exercise is so relaxing that you fall asleep. If that happens, don't be critical of yourself. If it happens frequently, see whether you can support being awake by placing a small pillow under your head, occasionally opening your eyes or perhaps even do the exercise seated rather than laying down.

When you are ready, direct your attention at your stomach and at the way it rises and falls as you breathe in and out. Follow the movement of the stomach and all sensations associated with it for a while.

Then bring your attention to the big toe on your left foot and observe what physical sensations are present. It is not about *thinking* about the sensations, but simply observing them. For example, the contact of the toe with the sock, a feeling of warmth or tingling, numbness or stiffness. If there is nothing to observe at that moment, that's fine too. You do not need to have a judgment about it. That's how it is in that moment. Move on to the other toes.

Then release your toes from your attention, and move it instead to the sole of the left foot. Again observe what physical sensations there are at the moment, with friendly curiosity. And then on to the top on the foot, the instep. Next to the heel and the ankle of the left foot. And, step by step, observe the sensations present, warmth, tingling, cold, prickles, touch...

When you have observed the whole foot, take the next in-breath, hold it in your attention in your mind and direct it in a friendly way towards the left foot. You allow, as it were, the breath to flow through the left foot from your body.

And then bring your attention to the left shin. There again you notice attentively what physical sensations are present. Take the time for this, for each part.

And so you go through the whole body: the left knee, the left thigh, then the right toes, the right foot, right shin, right knee, right thigh... Then the pelvis, the pubic area, buttocks, and hips. Abdomen and lower back, diaphragm, upper back, and chest...

Then you go to both hands at the same time. Observe the sensations in the thumbs and in the various fingers, the palm, the back of the hand, lower arms, elbow and upper arms... Shoulders, neck and the face (jaw, mouth, lips, nose, cheeks, ears, eyes, forehead) and finally to the head as a whole.

At each part of the body, you can stay for around 20 to 30 seconds with friendly attentiveness. You don't have to be precise or count. And if in a certain place you observe an intense sensation, you can "breathe there" and release the sensation as you breathe out so that some relaxation arises.

Your thoughts will, and that is certain, from time to time move in a different direction to where you are in your body with the exercise.

Notice this without making any judgment about it. That happens and it is very normal. If you notice it, pause for the moment that it happens and bring your attention back to the part of the body where you wanted to be at that moment.

Complete the exercise by slowly breathing through the whole body for a few minutes. Take time for this and observe how your body is one whole. Stand up in a calm way and take the feeling of mindfulness with you in the activities of the day.

Many of our participants express turmoil or "new" experiences with the body scan that they did not know.

"I couldn't lay still at all. I simply had to move."
"I had absolutely no feeling in my legs and that still won't appear, no matter how often I do it."
"I fall asleep right after my left leg and suddenly wake up when I'm somewhere around my chest. That's not the intention, is it?"
"How interesting. I injured my knee and since then I've never felt so many things in my right knee as during the body scan. There are apparently a lot of sensations there. I felt the pain and sorrow of that time rise to the surface again."
"I sometimes feel stiffness in my shoulders, but now this flowed away when I was there with my attention."

For many participants, the body scan is a considerable confrontation with reality. Managers are used to learning something practically and mentally, and as soon as they understand it, they want to master it immediately. The body scan is completely contrary to this. It starts with doing nothing, laying on a mat or cushion and only observing. Next, the body appears to be wanting to do its own thing and to become restless when it wants and not when its master wants it to. The body broadcasts signals that are experienced as unpleasant or unexpected and which sometimes evoke current or previous emotions. But unexpectedly it also leads to relaxation, when you pause on the experience of stiffness or tension.

The body scan also teaches that not every exercise has to be pleasant if you are to learn from it. Short-term results are not always self-evident. And it also teaches us how incredibly extensive and complex the networks of information exchange between body and mind are and that you sometimes have to rewire them or, in some areas, lay a completely new wiring.

In the event of it proving difficult, it is sensible not to be too hard on yourself and to distance yourself from thinking in terms or success or failure. Nor should you think that your body must always feel perfect and pleasing. If you observe pain or stiffness during the body scan, you shouldn't think that meditation doesn't work, because that reveals the assumption that meditation should lead to relaxation. But that is not the intention (although it can be a pleasant side effect). The intention is to train attention, the attentiveness. And then observing more or sometimes awkward signals is actually a sign of progress! What you can learn through the body scan is how your mind can cause turmoil in your body in a self-reinforcing process. And the reverse, that the body causes tension in the mind. By continually observing those tensions, you learn to realize that they can disappear or ease by paying attention to them. You only have to pay attention in a friendly manner.[9]

Many participants experience the body scan as a somewhat frustrating part of mindfulness training, that doesn't seem to produce immediate results. No relaxation, but an unexpectedly large and annoying number of signals. Yet there is profit to be had. There is, after all, nothing wrong if, frustrated, you discover that your body needs more rest and sleep and that you can allow that need instead of trying to suppress it. In addition, the body scan gives you insight into the doing mode. Pausing to observe your body and its signals shows how often you are sunk in thought or working on autopilot. And constantly attaching a judgment to everything, such as "am I doing this exercise perfectly or not" or "my body shouldn't feel like this" is such an aspect of the doing mode.

Pausing at the body's signals is an effective way of gaining insight into the doing mode and to repair the connection between body and mind as a system. Kabat-Zinn uses a wonderful word to describe the development of the physical self-feeling: *proprioception*. Some ob-

9 Ibid., 216-17.

servations of our body sensations come from touching other surfaces such as the chair on which we are sitting or the ground where we are standing. Other observations of the body, such as a sensation in your knee or of feeling your arm in space are directly linked with the body's awareness of itself. Repairing and increasing our proprioception makes us far more present in the world and we can use that presence in our actions. Synchronizing body and mind is the first step in developing the capacity for fearlessness. That doesn't mean that you will then be prepared to jump off a cliff or place your hand in the flames. No, fearlessness means that you can react to the situation around you with openness and precision. Making use of all your sensory abilities at the same time.[10]

Handling stress: stretching without striving

The impulse toward stress is almost constantly present in the life of a manager. The art is learning to cope with stress. Being able to make contact with the being mode, as we did in the previous exercises, is essential for this. Learning to switch mentally between doing mode and being mode is the next skill that resilient managers will have to master. Coping means that you learn to take your foot off the gas, take a step backwards and free yourself from an impulse or a thought. Our skill in switching is inhibited by our urge to perform. The mind tells us that we mustn't give up, that we can do it, and that the reward will be rich if we simply persevere. So push aside the signals of discomfort or limits. In the exercises of mindful movement, we learn to deal with limits in a different way: to play with them instead of breaching them. Exploring and testing instead of persisting without observing.

10 Chögyam Trungpa, *Shambhala. The Sacred Path of the Warrior* (Boston: Shambhala, 2007). 42.

Mindful movement[11]

You can start mindful movement in two ways: lying down or standing up. I shall describe them individually below. In both cases, it is important to take care of yourself and to allow the signals you receive from your body to weigh heavier than the instruction of the exercise. These are also exercises where you should consider whether you are physically capable of stretching and moving, for example, in the event of physical complaints or injuries. In that case, discussing these physical discomforts with your doctor or physiotherapist can be sensible. On the other hand, it is worth remembering that we are inclined to back away from a feeling of discomfort, while the value of these exercises is also in learning to deal with uncomfortable or awkward physical and mental reactions.

In many of the exercises with mindful movement, you reach at a given moment a physical or mental limit. Your first reaction may be to take a step back. Or exactly the opposite: to be tough and persevere. In both cases, you could try to explore the limit you encounter with a certain curiosity. What is it like if you keep your attention focused on the uncomfortable feeling as you stretch? Does the discomfort turn into a burning feeling? Does the tension ease? And what happens if you look at it in a friendly way and let your breathing relax? Much can be learned from the way you deal with the limits you encounter.

A word about your breathing during the execution of the movements. You breathe out as you make movements that contract your stomach and the front of your body. You breathe in as you make the front of your body bigger and contract the back. When the movement stops, continue with your normal breathing.

START LYING DOWN

In this case, lie down on your back on a mat or blanket on the floor (unless you have physical limitations that make lying flat impossi-

11 This description is based on: Jon Kabat-Zinn, *Handboek meditatief ontspannen* (Haarlem: Altamira-Becht, 2004). 121-32. ; Michael Chaskalson, *The Mindful Workplace* (Oxford: Wiley-Blackwell, 2011). 46-48. And the Teachers Manual of the training for mindfulness teachers from the Centrum voor Mindfulness (2009).

ble, then you can look for a different way). And become aware of the stream of your breath, in which the stomach rises and falls at each inhalation and exhalation.

Take the time to get to this position and to feel your complete body, from top to toe, the touch of the floor, the skin as the covering of the body.

And prepare yourself for the first reclining exercise.

a. Stretching exercise with arms and legs

Lay your arms alongside your body. Legs stretched out. Allow your attention to rest on your arms. Move both arms, stretched to the tip of the fingers, upwards and backwards along your head in the direction of the ground. Feel how far your arms can go, where they experience resistance and you notice that there is a limit. Keep your arms fully stretched.

Notice the stretching between the ribs and perhaps in the waist, notice the movement of the breath, keep the stomach loose and soft. Move your arms back and place them on the ground again.

Repeat the movement with your arms and at the same time stretch your legs by stretching them away from you along your heels. Your foot becomes perpendicular with your leg.

Feel the total stretching in your body and allow your breath to move freely in the stretching position in which you loosen your stomach. Hold the stretch for a moment and then move your arms back, allow the tension in your legs to relax slowly and rest.

Then notice where you are stretched and whether anything has changed.

b. Pelvis exercise

Your arms are on the ground, slightly away from your body. Bend the left knee and place your left foot flat on the floor. Now do this with your right knee. Both knees point towards the ceiling. Your feet are the width of your hips apart. And then, without losing the attentiveness for the whole body, allow your attention to rest on the area of the lower back, the area level with and below the waist. Notice whether anything has changed now that you are lying with your knees drawn up.

Move your lower body through the waist and push the area of the lower back into the ground. Feel how the hollow at the waist is now filled up and the stomach is pulled in. Notice how your hips tilt towards the ceiling as you make this movement.

Then move your lower body in the other direction so that the hollow appears in your waist and notice how the hips tilt the other way. Repeat both movements several times and feel whether the breath is moving freely. Does the upper body remain relaxed as you move your hips?

Finally, allow both legs to slip downwards so that you are once again in the starting position. Rest. Be conscious of your lower back... your waist. How does it feel there? Has anything changed? What physical sensations do you observe?

START STANDING UP

When you are ready, stand with your feet the width of your hips apart, your toes pointing forward. Relax your knees and bend them slightly. Hips bent slightly forward, your coccyx slightly pulled in. Your stomach may be soft, the chest open, the shoulders at rest and the arms hanging loosely alongside your body. You pull your chin in so that your neck is long.

Stand like this for a while and feel how your feet make contact with the floor. A position of being present, earthed, awake. You allow your breathing to go as it comes, all by itself. And focus your attention on your feet, notice from the inside how your feet make a footprint on the floor. Next, the attention goes via the ankles and the lower legs to the knees; notice whether these are tight or whether they can be made a little more loose. The attention goes farther upward to the hips, notice what is there. And if there is nothing to notice, notice that... Then the attention moves to the stomach, the diaphragm, it follows the spine. The attention is now on the shoulders, the arms that hang alongside the body. And then upwards via the neck, the skull to the crown of your head. And there you stand, from top to toe. Notice how your breath flows through the body... Rest.

a. Stretching of the arms

As you stand there, feel your feet on the ground, knees relaxed. With your next breath in, bring your arms forward and upward and breathe out. Notice the limit to which you can easily move your arms. Leave the shoulder blades low, do not pull up your shoulders. Feel how the body stretches while pushing your heels firmly into the ground. Keep stretching... breathe in and out calmly. Notice the stretching in the waist, the stomach and between the ribs. Lower the arms again and stand...

Raise both arms stretched to the side and upward to shoulder height and experience the great space in which the movements can take place. Your follow the movements very calmly and lightly with your attention. Turn your hands on your wrists until they point straight upward and notice the stretching in the arms. Now decide to push your arms from the shoulders even farther outward into the space without allowing them to become tense. It is as if you are feeling the space around them. Relax for a moment and then sense again, withdraw and stretch. Observe how your breathing reacts to this. Slowly lower your arms in the space around you. Feel that you are standing and observe the physical sensations that are present...

b. Raising leg sideways
To start, you stand with your feet at hips' width apart. In balance. During this exercise, you allow your eyes to rest on a fixed point straight ahead of you. Shift the weight of your body over your left leg and foot. Make that side strong by shifting your hip to straight above your leg; you notice that the muscles around your thigh, hip, and in your buttocks tighten. Raise both arms sideways to shoulder height and raise the right leg slightly sideways. Do this balance exercise quietly and patiently. Do not force the balance, but feel how your body organizes itself to support the weight of your body on one side. Observe how your breathing develops.
Return your leg to its starting position, lower your arms and become aware of the balance on two feet.
Then repeat on the other side, calmly and do it with careful attention. Then repeat each side again.
Finally you stand... stand... Observe the condition of your body...

The experiences participants have with mindful movement are highly diverse, from relaxing to confrontational, from fear of injury to insight into patterns of action when they reach a limit.

> *"I didn't pay any attention at all to the instruction to be careful. Noticed that I wanted to stretch as far as possible. I recognize that, going through the limits."*
>
> *"Two years ago, I suffered a severe back injury. My doctor told me to be careful. When I stretched my arm upward, I quickly brought it back down again. I felt something in my back and I was immediately frightened."*
>
> *"I noticed how much turmoil there is in my body. Kept on shaking when keeping balance. First I spoke strictly to myself: persevere! And suddenly I had to laugh about it..."*
>
> *"For me, this was a very relaxing exercise. And a lot easier than the body scan. Here, I could at least keep my attention focused."*

The exercises give us insight into attitudes that are frequently found in managers. The first is dealing with limits and being result-driven. What the exercise can teach you is how to deal with "soft" and "hard" limits and how to distinguish between them. You start to experience a soft limit at the moment your body is subjected to tension in the exercise. When you stretch your arms and then go a bit further, you notice that soft limit. Then you can naturally persist in order to achieve the aim – one which, at that moment, has been subtly changed by the mind from scouting the limits to pushing them as far as possible. But it is just as interesting to remain somewhat longer at that soft limit, to observe the physical sensations and signals from the body, to see how they develop and thus to search further for wider possibilities. Naturally there is also a hard limit, namely what the body can do at that moment.

Being result-driven often becomes so absolute that limits, even the hard ones, must be exceeded, no matter how. There is another way. Managers often discover how they force themselves through this exercise and they also pass on this attitude to their team or organization. The result is a hard performance culture, where you are held to account.

Stretching without striving teaches you that normal physical sensations sometimes arouse whole patterns of thoughts and awkward reactions. Persisting no matter what, always shying away at the first limit, being mentally angry with yourself – you name it. But if you can observe the sensations and thoughts without becoming entangled in them, you develop your own body-mind system into a valuable instrument for managing yourself and your team. You learn to cope with stress instead of just bearing it. And the wealth of signals and the recognition of your reaction pattern creates space and new possibilities for development.

In conversations you hold as manager this can be a very valuable instrument. A regular occurrence is that as manager you want something and the employee wants something else. Do you then persist in order to change it? And how do you feel in the discussion? You can't control the other's reaction. That's fortunate. But also awkward. What you can do is see your attitude in the conversation and adjust it. By observing the tension as a physical sensation, the conversation becomes more relaxed.

The art of pausing

Persisting is also typical for dealing with stress. Simply go the extra mile, is the motto. And so we exhaust ourselves and find ourselves in a negative spiral of stress. You can compare the moment of switching between doing and being with the conscious reaction to signals from soft limits. Very consciously scan them, pause for a moment, retreat very slightly and then investigate again, see whether we can go further. Surprisingly, there is generally more space than you first thought. We all experience that when, while stretching, we fix our breathing, a limit seems to have been reached. But if, through a small movement, we can allow our breathing to flow freely again, the stretch can sometimes reach another few centimeters. It can be as simple as that. If you deal with it like this, you learn to handle stress instead of just bearing it.

In your daily work as manager, switching can be rather difficult. The pressure to persist is strong, there is so much to be done. In mindfulness training, we therefore teach participants two exercises that support switching that are within reach for everybody at any time: the three-minute breathing space and the mindful check.

Three-minute breathing space

For this short exercise, sit up straight (or stand if that is better for you). A position of dignity, relaxation, the back straight but not stiff. Your attitude is alert and curious. You close your eyes.

Step 1: Becoming aware
Next, shift your attention to the inner experience and explore it with the question: what exactly am I experiencing at this moment?
- Which thoughts are going through my head? Observe them with your attention, recognize them as mental events.
- What feelings am I now experiencing? The attention includes them in the observation, whether they are pleasant, unpleasant, or neutral. They are there, you acknowledge them, and you don't need to change them.
- What physical observations are there? Where is there any tension, prickling, where is there stiffness, where comfort? Here again you explore your sensations with attention, without needing to change them.

Step 2: Focusing attention on breathing
Shift the attention to the breathing and the physical sensations associated with it. The stomach rises as you breathe in and falls as you breathe out. You follow with attention the whole movement inward and outward again. In this way, you anchor yourself in the here and now. And if your mind wanders, bring the attention in a friendly but firm way back to the breathing.

Step 3: Extending the attention
Next, extend the attention from following your breathing to the body as a whole. Including your pose, your expression, as if the whole body is breathing. If you notice sensations, they may be there, they are part of our body as a whole. In this way, a somewhat larger, more spacious awareness arises.
And then, finally, you open – when you are ready – your eyes again.[12]

12 There are many descriptions of the three-minute breathing space doing the rounds. This one is inspired by: Williams and Penman, *Mindfulness*: 142-43.

Personal check-in[13]

You can best do this exercise in a quiet environment. Perhaps close the door to your room, go to an empty conference room or a relaxation area where there is nobody else. Turn off the telephone. Lie down or stand up, and close your eyes.

Take the time to become quiet. Compliment yourself on the fact that you have taken this time.

You can do the exercise at the beginning of the day, before you start work. Or as an interlude, at any given moment.

Begin the mindful check-in by exploring the body and mind by sensing the stream of thoughts, emotions or physical sensations and briefly recording them in the attention. You do not need to do anything with them.

Perhaps this is the first break that you consciously take today in your busy schedule. And if you, for a moment, step out of doing mode and into being mode, you may notice how many sensations, emotions and thoughts move in your body-mind system.

You do not need to analyze everything now, or have a judgment about it or to work out how everything fits together. Simply allow yourself to be in the here and now, in the middle of everything that presents itself.

In this way, you check in with yourself. A few minutes. And compliment yourself that you have taken the time.

The limits of your availability

Keeping an eye open for all signals and knowing when to stop is also valuable for learning the limits of your availability as manager. People expect managers to be available to their people, but how far do you go in that? Always and everywhere, 24 hours a day, no rest from email, text messages, and chat? And how do you deal with caring for yourself. When do you take a rest, when is your time for recuperation? The well-developed body-mind instrument is at all times your valuable friend, who warns you in time.

13 Bob Stahl and Elisha Goldstein, *Mindfulness en stressreductie* (Amsterdam: Nieuwezijds, 2010). 27-28.

When stress rises too high or when you take too little time to de-stress. And then you can do a reality check by, for example, taking a breathing break. Pause and consider what you need now, as manager. And then go further with, for example, giving your employees greater clarity about your availability and the recovery time you need. And to include your recovery time in your schedule and lifestyle.

Sensing well instead of feeling good

Thinking belongs with doing. You quickly realize that when looking at what thinking is about: what are you going to do, how are you going to handle something, how can you do things differently etc. Feeling is observing what physical sensations and emotions you are dealing with: a headache, sadness, pleasure or anger, a stabbing pain, you name it. In mindfulness training, you learn to investigate it and gain insight into that. And then it is useful to define more sharply what it is all about: to feel, feelings, and emotions. What exactly are they?

Zen master Ritskes gives a good description of this in his recent book *Leer voelen wat je wilt voelen*.[14] He defines emotion as energy to act on behalf of the objectives for which you are consciously or unconsciously striving. If somebody has many emotions, that person apparently wants a lot. But it can lead to exhaustion, even though that person makes quite an energetic impression with their emotions. You run the risk of getting into difficulties with your emotions. They take control of you, you are swept along by them. With mindfulness you learn to give a conscious response to challenges, and thus use your drive in a more focused and effective way.

Then what is feeling? It's becoming aware of a physical reaction to something that happens in the body, in the mind, or in the environment. You may be sitting quietly on the sofa, and suddenly you think about something you have to do tomorrow. And your heart rate climbs: should I get up and write it down? You generally react at the same time with a reaction of desire or aversion: I would real-

---

14 Rients Ritskes, *Leer voelen wat je wilt voelen. Zenvol omgaan met emoties* (Rotterdam: Asoka, 2012). 39-55.

ly like to do it or would prefer not to do it. This is natural and you learn to recognize it in the training.

Insight into your own feelings and emotions helps you create a conscious response and to strengthen the ability to switch between being and doing. You can experience feelings and emotions, that is sensing or observing well or adequately. You don't need to do anything with it to feel good. It is about registering, and this releases you from a fixed reaction pattern.

It is important that we remember that everything we feel is a physical process. At the same time we know that mental processes can also conjure up feelings and emotions in our own mind. Just think of a vivid dream which generates a physical reaction, so that you wake up in a sweat. In Buddhism, thinking is considered one of our "sensory gates."[15] The better you learn how to feel, the easier the mental switching and the use of your emotional intelligence will become.

The difference between your thoughts and yourself: accepting and staying present

You have already learned how to gain insight into the autopilot of the doing mode. First, by allowing experiences from your senses to enter, by learning to use the signals from your body, and by learning to switch mentally using stretching without striving. You have learned to direct your attention at observing experiences. And that you can be consciously present in everyday life without being dragged along on autopilot into a spiral of stress, which is in turn fed by the thought that, as manager, you must always be available.

We are now going to strengthen the power of attentiveness by focusing on two key exercises in mindfulness training: sitting and walking meditation. With these exercises, you get a better insight into the operation of the mind and how it influences your actions. You learn to free yourself from the identification with your thought world. You learn to see how you deal with your experiences, how you push them away in aversion or attach to them if you don't want to lose them.

15 Ibid., 130.

Sitting meditation

Take time to assume a sitting position. That can be on a cushion generally placed on a mat. Or on a sturdy chair, where you can sit upright. If you sit on a chair, make sure you sit with your back straight and normally, which means you do not lean against the back of the chair. If you sit on a cushion on the floor, see whether you can get your knees as close to the floor as possible or even touch it. By doing this, your hips tilt forward. Generally, you can't do that immediately but it will get better with practice. You can vary the height of the cushions or use a meditation bench. See whether you can sit comfortably and whether you feel well supported. If you have a disability or injury, adjust the position and choose the position that is safe and comfortable for you and which supports you in order to be present from moment to moment. That could even be reclining, if necessary.

The position you adopt when sitting is also important, both the physical position and the inner attitude. Your back should be straight, not stiff and also not tense. Your head relaxed and straight, your shoulders hanging loose. A position that exudes dignity, just as a queen would sit on her throne. You can lay your hands in your lap, folded, or lay them on your legs, palms open towards the ceiling, if that feels pleasant to you. The inner attitude is one of curiosity and a light but not tense alertness. Open for what is going to come.

Breathing

Direct the attention to your breathing. Most people find it easiest to follow the in and out movement of breathing by watching how the stomach goes up and down. When breathing in through the nose or mouth, the breath goes through the windpipe to the chest and the stomach rises; when breathing out the movement goes in the opposite direction. It can prove helpful to get the rise and fall more sharply etched in your memory by laying your hands on your stomach and following the movement. And you can also follow the breath by mentioning softly "rising" and "falling" in your thoughts. The advantage of the breathing movement is that it is always present. It is a natural movement of the body. It is not necessary to get this movement under control, you simply have to follow it. It doesn't have to be faster or slower. The breathing is and is allowed to be what it is.

The attention wanders
It is very usual that you notice your attention wandering. Suddenly your thoughts are on something else and no longer on your breathing. A plan suddenly flashes through your mind, or you think of your task list. You drift off or think back to yesterday with pleasure. Don't think that this is wrong. It simply happens and is an attribute of the mind. Exactly the moment you notice that your attention has wandered is actually very beautiful, for that means that you realize it. You are aware of what you experience at that moment. And that is the attentiveness you are training.

What you do at that moment is to bring your attention back in a friendly but firm way to observing how your stomach rises and falls. And then you simply go on following your breathing movement.

It will often happen that the attention of the mind wanders again. You should not consider this a failure, even though it might be frustrating to notice that you do not have your mind under control. The advantage is that you learn to look at it as something that happens. That can help you practice patience. And it helps you anchor yourself in the here and now, time and again.

Physical sensations
Once you have followed the rising and falling of your stomach for a while, you can then direct the attention to observing the physical sensations in the body. Perhaps the first thing to demand attentiveness is the contact of the buttocks with the cushion or the chair or of the knees and feet with the floor. You can then allow the attention to rest on the body as a whole, from feet to crown. Physical sensations such as an itch, warmth or cold, tingling or prickling, stiffness and tension or suppleness, hardness or softness of a spot in the body may intrude. You follow the physical sensations in the body with attention.

You may perhaps notice that the physical sensations evoke a certain sentiment. One sensation feels pleasant, another unpleasant, and yet another is neutral in character. Notice that one is no better than the other, but that you may have the inclination to make such a judgment in your thoughts. Perhaps you can look with amazement and a fresh view at each physical sensation and observe it, including the associated sentiment but without passing any judgment.

If you have sat for a while, it is possible that a certain physical sensation continues longer and moves much more strongly to the foreground of your attention. You can respond to such a dominant sensation in two ways. One way is to do something about it: you can scratch an itch, for example. If you do that, you can do it with full attention. Observe the intention in yourself to do something and carry out the action attentively. And observe the effects of the action. The other method is to do nothing and only remain with your attention on the physical sensation. You take your attention to it and follow the development of the sensation. Does it become stronger or weaker, does the character change, does it, perhaps, disappear.

And in this way you follow the physical sensations in the body. And here again your attention may regularly wander. If it does, bring it back in a friendly but firm way to observing the physical sensations and the associated feelings of pleasant, unpleasant, or neutral. Again and again.

Sounds

Once you have spent some time with your attention focused on breathing and on physical sensations, you can shift your attention to observing sounds. Sounds can come from inside the body or from outside. What you notice is perhaps a loud sound or maybe a soft, sharp or dull sound, with a high or low tone. Whatever you hear, there is no need to interpret it; you do not need to trace where it came from or what caused it. You can simply notice it as sound, nothing more.

Nor do you need to search for sounds, just let them come to you.

And perhaps observe that you register sounds and form a judgment about them. Then let go of the sound you heard until you notice the following sound. And so on...

Thoughts

Now shift your attention from observing sounds to the following area of attentiveness, observing thoughts. Thoughts constantly pass through your mind. Sometimes it is a long train of thoughts and associations, sometimes just a flash. Now they last long, now short. Sometimes very vague, then suddenly razor sharp. There are all sorts of thoughts.

What you do is observe the thoughts. What type of thought emerges now? And then you let go of that thought without bothering about the content. You let go of the thought again.

You could see thoughts as clouds that move across the sky and you are lying there looking at them. Some clouds drift past slowly, others rush past. Some are large and complex, others are small. Sometimes they cover the sky, sometimes there is just one small cloud. You do not need to do anything with your thoughts. You don't need to make them pass faster or to stop them altogether. You look at your thoughts without identifying yourself with them. You can see them as individual events that arise in the mind and then pass away.

Emotions

The following area of attentiveness is that of emotions. Thoughts often induce emotions, they have an emotional charge. Your mood changes and you can also observe that. You hit on an emotion, for example happiness, sorrow, fatigue, or boredom. Look at which catches your attention.

You observe them with your attention and then let them go again. And each time the attention wanders, whether it is while observing thoughts or emotions, you observe that in a friendly way, without judging yourself or seeing it as a failure or mistake. It is what it is. And then you bring the attention in a friendly but firm way back to observing your thoughts or emotions from moment to moment.

Choiceless awareness

We have now seen all the areas of attention when sitting: breathing, physical sensations and the associated feeling, sounds, thoughts, and emotions. A multitude of experiences that could possibly present themselves to our attentiveness. We can now direct our attention to observing what is in the foreground here and now without focusing on a certain area. It can be a sound, a thought, a physical sensation, a sentiment, an emotion, or whatever presents itself at that moment. We call that random attention.

You allow your attention to rest on whatever it notices and then you release it until the next thing presents itself. And so on.

If the attention has wandered during the period of random awareness, you can redirect it in a friendly but firm way to observing what is being presented at that moment in the field of attentiveness. If that proves troublesome, you can always redirect your attention to your breathing. Your breathing is the ever present anchor for attentiveness and for stabilizing the attention. You can then shift from giving attention to your breathing back to random awareness.

Conclusion

For the last period of the (extended) sitting meditation, you can again direct the attention to the movement of the breathing. You follow the rise and fall of the stomach and gently note that rise and fall in your thoughts. You sit like this for several minutes until you finish the sitting meditation.

Two things stand out in the experiences of participants of the training: discovering just how many thoughts are constantly generated by our mind and the inner struggle that we wage with the thoughts that pass by.

> *"I had no idea that so many thoughts pass through me. It's like a waterfall; they keep on coming. Wave after wave, without stopping…"*
> *"Difficult to get to see my thoughts. They keep slipping away when I try to observe them. That is a lot easier with physical sensations."*
> *"I notice that I am constantly fighting with my thoughts. I really don't want to see them. I actually find them rather annoying."*
> *"I simply can't let go of a thought. I'm completely absorbed by it. And then I have to strictly address myself."*
> *"I simply can't empty my head. Those thoughts keep on coming…"*
> *"I couldn't do it, stop wandering and observe thoughts. And then it seemed as if my body relaxed and it made me cheerful. Wonderful. But suddenly it was gone and I found that annoying. I became angry. And I suddenly had to think of my father when he read the newspaper in the evening and I didn't get any attention from him. I came over all hot."*

When we observe our thoughts – and the same applies for physical sensations and sounds – we soon notice that we cannot exercise any control over them. And that can easily irritate us. The stream of thoughts goes on and on and we can't stop it. We also call that the waterfall of thoughts. What we can learn here is to stand just behind the waterfall and allow the thoughts to pass by. Learn to look at the drops and waves. Jon Kabat-Zinn makes a nice analogy with surfing: you can't stop the waves but you can learn to surf. You could see this stream of thoughts as the doing mode of the mind. You learn the being mode by freeing yourself from it.

That, incidentally, is not that easy because our natural reaction to experiences is to reject, avoid, or hang on to them.[16] When we reject an experience, we react with absence or boredom. Don't feel like it now, is the message or: not again, we've already had that. And in our head we concern ourselves with other things. We avoid an experience by suppressing it, we get angry at it: "I don't want this experience!" Or we drift away to a more pleasant experience, a delicious day dream: "wouldn't it be great to lay on the beach now." The third option is to hang on to the experience, certainly when it is pleasant: "I'm so enjoying writing, I want to keep the flow, wonderful." And you know that, at that very moment, you've already lost it...

What we do is push away the experience instead of observing it and remaining with it. Learning to remain with it, even when the experience is unpleasant, is an important skill for developing resilience. Remaining with it assumes acceptance and that is a term the participants often find unpleasant. Acceptance evokes an association with resignation. Mindfulness is not intended for accepting everything, they shout in chorus. What is interesting is that acceptance demands an *active* action and is thus the reverse of resignation. Acceptance means that you purposely *permit* experiences and try for the moment to do nothing about them. So you actively prevent the three reactions of rejection, avoidance, and retention described above and allow the experience. Just as, with the sitting meditation, we move with our attention toward a dominant phys-

16 Zindel V. Segal, J. Mark G. Williams, and John D. Teasdale, *Aandachtgerichte cognitieve therapie bij depressie* (Amsterdam: Uitgeverij Nieuwezijds, 2006). 203.

ical experience and look at its development. And that is the reverse of resignation, which tends toward passivity and impotence. With acceptance, you have to exert some energy. You register the experience before you decide what you do with it.

The importance of acceptance and staying with the experience is that you learn the skill of breaking free from the mental switching of the autopilot. Without acceptance of what the experience is, whether it is a pleasant, unpleasant, or neutral experience, you won't be able to do that.

Walking meditation[17]

In walking meditation, you concentrate on the walking itself. You can focus on placing your foot as a whole or on certain elements of the movement – such as changing feet, moving, placing the foot, change again; or on the movement of your whole body. You can combine attentive walking with attentive breathing.

For some people, it is extremely difficult to meditate sitting down, but if they walk, meditation takes place almost by itself. Whoever you are, sitting down all the time is impossible. And some people simply cannot manage to sit attentively with the pain, turmoil and anger they are feeling. But they can manage that when walking.

Walking is just as good as sitting. What is important is what you focus internally. If you meditate while walking, your goal is not to reach a certain place. You only walk along a path, back and forth or round and round. It is about the challenge of being completely present for each step, for each breath.

The exercise means that you take every step for what it is and that you remain fully attentive to that step. That means you must feel what it is like to walk – in your feet, your legs, your poise, and your gait, and as always from moment to moment and in this case also from step to step.

Just as in sitting meditation, everything will arise to distract your at-

17 Based on: Kabat-Zinn, *Handboek meditatief ontspannen*: 133-38. And on: Frits Koster, *Basisprincipes Vipassanā-meditatie* (Rotterdam: Asoka, 2008). 25-29.

tention from the simple experience of walking. We work with those observations, thoughts, feelings, impulses, memories, and prospects that present themselves during walking in the same way as in sitting meditation.

Take the time and space for this exercise. You can best practice walking meditation in a place where you will not attract the attention of others.

Stand up. Close your eyes for a moment. Focus your full attention on standing. Go with your attention along your legs to your feet. Notice how your feet make contact with the floor. Check out the rest of your body: your spine, your head upright on your body. Your arms relaxed along your side. Then open your eyes again, and direct them straight ahead without looking at anything specific.

When you start to walk, see whether you can walk slower than normal, with slightly shorter steps. This will allow you to be more aware of the movement.

And before you actually start moving, you can first of all feel the intention to move. It is as if we make the movement in our mind before we actually take it.

Then slowly raise your right foot and step forward... and now your left foot... and your right again. And you can register each movement as: right goes like this, left like this.

If other objects or experiences are present in a slight way, you do not need to pay them any specific attention. You can simply continue walking.

If something clearly arises in the foreground, for example a pain or a stitch, something that catches your eye, a strong emotion or thought, do not consider this a disturbance. Notice it, briefly pay attention to it, and then return to registering your movement.

Perhaps, as you walk, you can allow your attention to dissect the process of walking – register it even more precisely. You can, for example, do that by subdividing the movement into "raising," "moving forward" and "placing it on the floor." You register: "raise," "proceed" and "place." And then the other foot.

Perhaps you can also become aware of how the weight of your body shifts from one foot to the other. Register this as: "descending," "standing" and "coming free." In addition, allow your attention to notice your instep, your ankles, and your calves. And register which bones and muscles are doing all the work to make this movement possible.

And then you come slowly to rest again. Stand. Perhaps you would like to close your eyes for a moment. How does your body feel now? Are there thoughts, feelings? Let the effect of this exercise slowly take effect on you.

In addition to acceptance, an important learning experience of the sitting and walking meditation is that you really can free yourself from your thoughts. The moment that people discover that they are not their thoughts but that they have thoughts is, for many, a real eye-opener. The first time that they become aware that their identity does not depend on the stream of thoughts into which they are sucked. Thoughts appear not to be *the* truth or the whole reality, they are not facts.

If we succeed in treating thoughts in this way, space arises for a different thinking, for the conscious response of the mental switching and the open mindset we encountered in the previous chapter. Kabat-Zinn suggests that the core is that, while meditating, we treat all our thoughts equally, without suppressing them. It is not about the quantity of thoughts that you have, and so your head does not have to be empty. It is about: "how much place do you make for them from moment to moment in your field of consciousness in order to allow them to have a place." By recognizing your thoughts as thoughts, you can begin to see sharper what is going on and this allows a greater space for choice in your life. You free yourself from the distorted reality often created by thoughts.[18]

18 Kabat-Zinn, *Handboek meditatief ontspannen*: 88-89.

The mindful manager: resilience and an open mind

Developing mindfulness as manager is a learning process. Learning ensures that an experience, a moment consciously lived in the here and now, can influence your future behavior. With mindfulness, you learn to approach this here and now moment with an open mind. That offers you the possibility of consciously choosing between action and reflection. It offers you resilience. Below are the elements from which the resilience of the mindful manager is constructed:

1. Greater attentiveness, because you learn to play with your attention and know where it is and learn to consciously bring back your attention in the moment.
2. Greater resilience, you are better equipped against the pressure of work and the turmoil around you. You learn to better determine the limits of your own availability and the balance between work and private life.
3. Greater emotional intelligence, because you learn to use not only the mental signals but all other signals of the sensory experience.
4. Great clarity of mind, because you are less easily dragged along by thoughts, emotions and feelings. You can then choose a conscious response and no longer allow yourself to be swept along in an automatic reaction.
5. Greater ability to switch between action and reflection, with which you can better steer your team and your organization.

Just take a look at the experiences of participants in our mindfulness training for managers:

> *"I notice that I am developing a different energy management system. Less stressed."*
> *"I see that I react more consciously."*
> *"I make use of my emotions rather than be controlled by them."*
> *"I look with a broader view, each new day with a flesh look. Take time for rest and can listen better."*
> *"My attention for the group was reasonably good but now I can*

combine that with attention for myself. That makes it stronger."
"Now that I react more calmly, the people in my team do the same."
"We observe much quicker what is taking place emotionally in our team and do something with it."
"Thinking with more awareness, doing with more awareness. In practice, I am less frequently constricted by certain circumstances, can put things better into perspective."
"I succeed rather well in being a beacon of calm in these turbulent times of organizational change. Surprising, as my own job is on the line."
"We are better able to distinguish between main and secondary issues and concentrate better on things."
"I am increasingly better able to think: must I do this task? Must I do it now? Instead of turning head over heels to do everything myself, and right now!"
"Silence. We simply take the time and our creativity increases."
"I feel more calm and space in my head. Not react primarily, but observe more and react from this attitude. Or perhaps not even react at all."

By training mindfulness, you learn to act with a greater presence of mind. That seems at odds with the image that we frequently have of meditation as being immersed in peace and quiet and the absence of thoughts. Meditation then seems to be something which totally absorbs you, just as you can experience with making music or running. That may seem so from the outside, but then you are really missing the point. Because meditation is very active and conscious. It is not about sitting in a flow, having no thoughts or freeing yourself from all physical experiences. Meditation is actually exercising with an alert mind by *being aware of what you are doing while you are doing it.* Meditating is not concerned with the content or the extent of your experiences. Sometimes there are many, sometimes few. Meditating is not about the experience itself, but about the relationship with your experience. Are you swept along with it or do you choose to react consciously to it? Can you accept every experience and let it be, do you notice whether you resist the experience or wish to clamp onto it? By noticing every experience, you also free yourself from it. Identifying with your experiences stops at the same moment. And space arises for free and conscious action. Here is the alertness or presence of mind that you develop in the process of meditating. In four steps, you teach yourself to use your mind in a new, open way.[19]

Steps to an open mind

1. You observe that the mind is not where you want it to be

2. You free it from this

3. Direct it at where you want it to be

4. And you are able to remain there with your mind

In Buddhism, these steps are also called the four forms of proper effort,[20] because you can go with an open mind from a harmful to a beneficial situation. You learn to direct your thinking rather than allow yourself to be dragged along on autopilot. And so you can act effectively.

Kabat-Zinn once compared it to surfing. You can't do anything about the waves, about their number, their height or their power. But you can learn to surf, see, and feel what is coming at you and freely deal with it. That is mindful and therefore effective management.

Appendix: the learning process of mindfulness

The learning process of mindfulness takes place according to Kolb's well-known model of experiential learning, which, he says himself, can be used well in mindfulness and thus is strengthened by it.[21] The model is strongly investigative and thus fits the ap-

---

19 Chaskalson, *The Mindful Workplace*: 93.

20 Frits Koster, *Het web van wijsheid* (Rotterdam: Asoka, 2005). 231. This is about effort: a. to remove a harmful state of mind; b. to prevent a harmful state of mind occurring; c. to develop a beneficial state of mind; d. to cultivate further beneficial states of mind.

21 Baubeck Yeganah and David A. Kolb, "Mindfulness and Experiential Learning," *OD Practitioner* 41, no. 3 (2009).

proach of the Buddha with his "only trust what you yourself experience as true." The learning model of Kolb is as follows:

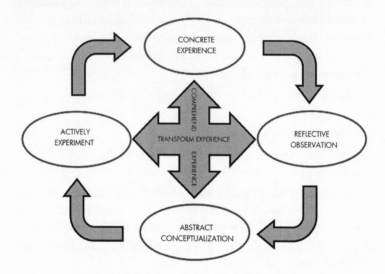

Learning starts with gaining an experience. We then explore that experience in the second step. Kolb calls that reflective observation. Normally we are inclined to place an experience into a category or pigeonhole it. With the stage of exploration or reflective observation, we postpone that for a while and take the time to look at the experience on its own merits. Letting it be what it is. With this, space for a fresh look at the experience also arises. You learn by not knowing. Then we connect the experience with what we already know, with abstract concepts we have at our disposal. Have we had this experience previously, which new aspects does it have, does it lead to a different interpretation of the experience? Thus we gain insight into the context, but also the space to place the experience in a new context or against a different background. An experience that you always become angry and erupt if somebody criticizes you, and in which you think "that's just the way I am" can become an experience in which you see your anger coming and recognize it and let it go again. And so a new context arises: "I do not necessarily have to do anything when I feel anger" and thus there is room for new behavior. And the fourth step is then precisely trying out the new possibility. Learning mindfulness takes place in the same way.

Learning cycle and mindfulness practices

Stage learning cycle	Mindfulness practices
Specifically experiencing	• Attention for breathing and relaxation of the body
	• Attention for all sorts of sensory experiences, so that your mindset becomes open and the autopilot is disengaged
Reflective observation	• Become aware of the impulse to act
	• Postpone the impulsive thoughts and actions through breathing and acceptance
	• Sitting meditation in which your attention remains on your thoughts and feelings instead of doing something with them
	• Practicing recognition and acceptance instead of judging
Abstract conceptualization	• Open the assumptions that you make at this moment to discussion
	• View the perspective of others
	• Dare to doubt your own "truth"
	• See shades of grey instead of digital thinking
Actively experiment	• Pose new questions: change the conversation by asking questions that generate possibilities
	• Thinking about thoughts and behaviors that you admire in another in a certain situation and trying them out
	• Experiment by reacting to events and people differently than usual

There are mindfulness practices at each stage of the learning cycle which support the learning process and which you are able to learn for this.[22]

For every person, one type of exercise will be easier than the others; we all have our own preference for a certain learning style that matches a certain stage. But our learning will be most effective if we go through all the stages. The use of mindfulness exercises can help managers and organizations to strengthen the learning processes in their organizations.

22 Ibid., 12.

References

Brandsma, Rob. *Mindfulness basisboek. Kennis, achtergrond en toepassing.* Houten: LannooCampus, 2012.

Chaskalson, Michael. *The Mindful Workplace.* Oxford: Wiley-Blackwell, 2011.

Kabat-Zinn, Jon. *Coming to Our Senses.* New York: Hyperion, 2005.

————. *Handboek meditatief ontspannen.* Haarlem: Altamira-Becht, 2004.

Koster, Frits. *Basisprincipes Vipassanā-Meditatie.* Rotterdam: Asoka, 2008.

————. *Het web van wijsheid.* Rotterdam: Asoka, 2005.

Ritskes, Rients. *Leer voelen wat je wilt voelen. Zenvol omgaan met emoties.* Rotterdam: Asoka, 2012.

Segal, Zindel V., J. Mark G. Williams, and John D. Teasdale. *Aandachtgerichte cognitieve therapie bij depressie.* Amsterdam: Uitgeverij Nieuwezijds, 2006.

Siegel, J. Daniel. *Mindsight. The New Science of Personal Transformation.* New York: Bantam Books, 2010.

Silsbee, Doug. *The Mindful Coach.* San Francisco: Jossey-Bass, 2010.

Stahl, Bob, and Elisha Goldstein. *Mindfulness en stressreductie.* Amsterdam: Nieuwezijds, 2010.

Trungpa, Chögyam. *Shambhala. The Sacred Path of The Warrior.* Boston: Shambhala, 2007.

Williams, Mark, and Danny Penman. *Mindfulness.* Amsterdam: Nieuwezijds, 2011.

Yeganah, Baubeck, and David A. Kolb. "Mindfulness and Experiential Learning." *OD Practitioner* 41, no. 3 (2009): 8-14.

4

Mindfully managing teams

> " 'Saving the world' is so hard [...] that it is not likely to be
> sustainable. Instead, it is more skilful to focus on developing
> inner peace, compassion, and aspiration. When [those] are all
> strong, compassionate action comes naturally and organically,
> and hence, it is sustainable."[1]
>
> Chade-Meng Tan, Google's Jolly Good Fellow
> (which nobody can deny) – *Search Inside Yourself*

In this chapter, I will show you how you can mindfully manage a
team. Before doing that, I shall first consider what a good team is.
In my view that is a team that works with full awareness. You can
increase the team's effectiveness by creating a *green zone of mind-fulness* where switching between action and reflection, between
doing and being is guaranteed within the team. Mutual resilience
is part of this, as are the development of the emotional intelligence
in the group, mindful communication through dialogue, and a
compassionate performance culture.

Mindful management means taking the lead in creating that
green zone by setting the example and establishing the attitude in
which performances can be delivered: assuming responsibility for
each other, being unrelentingly honest, and productively compas-sionate. With this you create the basis for a team, organization or
network that does not function on autopilot but knows what it is
doing.

---

1 Chade-Meng Tan, *Search Inside Yourself* (New York: HarperCollins,
2012). 241.

Successful teams and the green zone of mindfulness

Every team begins with a shared aspiration. A fire-fighting team has the ambition to protect us against fires or if they should nevertheless occur, to keep the consequences to the absolute minimum. A team of developers at a software company wants to make the very best apps for smartphones. The teachers at a school want to ensure that the children receive a good education.

The importance of such an aspiration cannot be underestimated. It is the adhesive between people in a team. For we know by now that external stimuli, such as monetary rewards, no longer motivate us in the 21st century and that we must access our internal sources of motivation. People wish to make a meaningful and significant contribution to customers and stakeholders.[2]

The living presence of a strong performance ethos based on that aspiration is therefore logical. Everybody in the team strives resolutely towards joint results both for customers, employees, and stakeholders. And, at the same time, that ethos increases the motivation for learning and the growth of employees.[3] Successful teams have all this at their disposal. But it frequently goes wrong with aspirations when they are set out by management as rigid targets and hang like the sword of Damocles above the head of each individual employee. In such a cut-throat culture, you see team members throw in the towel because they no longer feel connected to the aspiration.

In addition to keeping the aspirations sharp without falling into unattainable ambitions or rigid focus on objectives, teams also need an excellent way of collaborating. The essence of this is not that teams have the right technical or functional skills, but more importantly that they are good at solving problems and communicating among themselves:[4] they can listen carefully to each oth-

---

2 Daniel H. Pink, *Drive* (Amsterdam: Business Contact, 2010). Also see: Dave Ulrich and Wendy Ulrich, *Het waarom van werk. Naar een organisatie van overvloed* (Amsterdam: Business Contact, 2011).

3 Jon R. Katzenbach and Douglas K. Smith, *Het geheim van teams. Een organisatie van wereldklasse creëren* (Schiedam: Scriptum, 1997). 173-80.

4 Ibid., 55.

er, they give each other the benefit of the doubt, express constructive criticism, support each other, and recognize each other's
performances and input.

In such a team, it is clearly not just about the results. There is also the awareness that you must do things together and that it matters how you do them together. In such a team, you will see that
people have assumed various leadership and social roles and that
you, as manager, are not the only one giving directions. One person is good at asking questions, the other at interpreting events
without prejudice, and others at giving people space. Together this
distribution of roles ensures that attention is well directed within
the team and that there is confidence in each other.[5]

I notice whether a team is working well from the way I feel myself: at ease. I talk as easily with team members about things at home
as about issues that crop up at work. In one team I led, I noticed this
from the ease with which matters were picked up by others. As
manager, I had to do virtually no managing. Constructive criticism
(but by no means less critical or penetrating) is given by everybody
on proposals on how to address things, and the evaluation is just as
vigorous, with no regard for person or status. Nobody tried a cover
up and nobody was inclined to defend themselves.

But in those places where this doesn't work well, you see the
hedgehog effect, as INSEAD professor and leadership specialist,
Manfred Kets de Vries, calls it. Team members keep a distance from
each other because collaboration evokes too much insecurity.[6] They
shut themselves off from each other and they do not succeed in
exposing their weaknesses, because they do not wish to embarrass
themselves or feel guilty. Such a team does not get much further than
the usual planned progress discussions and team meetings under the
chairmanship of the manager. It falls into the ritual of the Monday
morning agenda. And you find *mindless* communication there,
which is really only about protecting or promoting self interest.[7]

5   Ibid., 64.

6   Manfred Kets de Vries, *Het egel effect* (Den Haag: Academic Service,
    2012).

7   Susan Chapman, *The Five Keys to Mindful Communication* (Boston:
    Shambhala, 2012). 17.

In good teams, you also see that team members take responsibility for their own actions and for those of each other as a team: "we hold ourselves accountable for achieving these results and this way of working." That is going a step further than saying that your manager can hold you to account. In that case, it is something that is outside the team. The question of whether you, as a team, will accept the *joint* responsibility for the agreed results is really crucial.[8]

If that doesn't succeed, then you often see a pattern of shirking responsibility, of shifting the burden for solving a problem to a group of specialists in the team or the managers, or placing it outside the team, as often happens with government policy. The pattern of shirking responsibility is, in addition, a pattern of choosing short-term solutions over taking the time and the effort to find qualitatively better, innovative solutions.[9]

So it isn't all that easy to build up and maintain a successful team. For that you need aspirations, we-communication and taking responsibility. You easily fall into a trap in one of these three areas: a rigid pressure to perform, ego-driven collaboration, or shirking of responsibilities.

Mindfulness helps you, as manager, to tip the balance in the right direction. If, as manager, you learn to shift between action and reflection, you can also help your team direct its attention properly. That is because, as manager, you have a *"contagious"* role in the team, your mood, and your actions influence the whole group.[10] People look to leaders to set the course, the direction, and also the mood, for much communication is non-verbal. A leader's attitude can have a far-reaching influence on the mood.

With your attitude and behavior, you can help team members

8 Katzenbach and Smith, *Het geheim van teams. Een organisatie van wereld-klasse creëren*: 67-68.

9 Peter Senge, *De noodzakelijke revolutie* (Den Haag: Academic Service, 2009). 16-17.

10 Daniel Goleman, Richard Boyatzis, and Annie McKee, *Primal Leader-ship. Realizing the Power of Emotional Intelligence* (Boston: Harvard Business School Press, 2002).

stay connected with the aspirations instead of the urge to perform. You can also help in developing a greater performance capacity by strengthening the emotional intelligence and with it better communications. For mindfulness helps unmask ingrained reaction patterns and encourages experimental actions. Such a team, whether it operates within an organization or a network of organizations, succeeds in conquering the mutual restraint and helps people really work together. Mindfulness, as I wrote in chapter three, generates not only insight but also connectedness. And that makes it easy to empathize with your team members and to take responsibility for each other and for the way you collaborate. Through mindfulness, you learn to deal more easily with the relationships with your team members, because you see what has been caused by your autopilot and you can consciously cope with that. Exercising mindfulness also influences the strengthening of the moral and ethical awareness for what is present in the organization and with the stakeholders, and increases corporate social responsibility.[11]

With these three aspects of successful teams in the back of our minds, we can now describe the difference between a team that works mindfully and uses the ability to switch between action and reflection to the full extent and a team in which the autopilot rules the internal collaboration. These are the aspects to which you, as a mindful manager, can give direction.

I call a team that operates on full awareness a team with a *green zone of mindfulness*.[12] A green zone, where switching between action and reflection is raised to an art form. By smart and timely switching, such a team can better cope with stress and burn-out is

11 Juliet Adams, "The business case for mindfulness in the workplace: a guide to promoting mindfulness to corporate clients," (Mindfulnet.org, 2012). And also: Nicole E. Ruedy and Maurice E. Schweitzer, "In the Moment: the Effect of Mindfulness on Ethical Decision Making," *Journal of Business Ethics* 95 (2010).

12 The term "green zone" is inspired by the work of Susan Chapman about mindful communicating, but I apply it more broadly, namely to mindful teamwork. See: Chapman, *The Five Keys To Mindful Communication*: xiv.

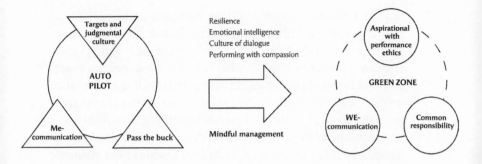

prevented. There, emotional intelligence is used to the full in order to collaborate better. There, mutual communication is safe and there is no hard performance culture or a culture of fear. There, performing goes hand in hand with learning, because there is compassion for each other. Team members and the manager empathize with each other and take responsibility for the joint results, even though it is necessary to hold each other to quality and agreements, or to the necessary change process of the other and yourself, or the team.

Below, I discuss the most important dimensions of the green zone of mindful teamwork which you can use as manager: resilience, emotional intelligence, mindful communication through a culture of dialogue, and compassionate performance. You will find a short explanation for each dimension, with exercises you can do as manager or with your team.

Resilience in your team

Every team requires a considerable degree of robustness or resilience if it is to be capable of handling tension. For in every organization, periods of hectic activity alternate with moments of slower pace and in many cases it even appears as if teams only operate under high pressure and no single process runs according to the rules. If that is the case, it is the task of the manager to offer support to the employees.

Robustness is the degree to which a team can absorb disruptions and recuperate itself.[13] Still perform even under pressure or in bad conditions without endangering health. Bend with an inconvenient event, but then spring back so that the situation recovers, and learn from that.[14] With a mindfulness-based approach, you avoid employees coming into the spiral of self-sacrifice which we described earlier. Attention for the health of your employees is the starting point for this and exercising mindfulness offers many opportunities of learning to better cope with stress and so keep the health of your team up to scratch. You could do the resilience check below for yourself or with your team:

The resilience check: how robust is your team?
- How often do you take a step back in your team?
- How is the health of your team members and the team as a whole?
- How do you deal with success and failure?
- How often do you choose for a moment of silence and reflection?
- Do you doggedly accept everything or do you talk about things?
- How do you react to the workload: go the extra mile or take time to move down a gear when the job is done?

Space for resilience means that you, as manager, ensure an ambiance of safety. Safety so that team members can get what concerns them off their chest, without being called to account for it. The encouragement, in fact, to look well and to observe and to share the information with each other. A resilient team is a team in which the uncertainty to which it is exposed through work and changes is not hidden away behind toughness, but is freely discussed.

Research shows that mindfulness can make an important contribution to organizing this type of resilience. Meditating for fif-

---

13 Andrew Price, *Slow Tech. Manifesto for an Overwound World* (London: Atlantic Books, 2009). 140.

14 Karl E. Weick and Kathleen M. Sutcliffe, *Managing the Unexpected* (San Francisco: John Wiley & Sons, 2010). 71.

teen minutes a day at work, seated in your chair, does a lot of good in itself.[15] Some companies create special quiet areas or meditation rooms. Trade unions too argue for these possibilities in negotiations about employment conditions.[16] In the organization, a culture emerges in which there is attention for resilience, in which there is permission to make space for this, and in which teams and management stimulate each other in this and take the responsibility for it. One of the ways to do that is using the following resilience meditation, which you can do on your own or with your team (why not guide the exercise yourself?):

Resilience meditation[17]
Take fifteen minutes for the following exercise; choose a place where you will not be disturbed. Sit on a chair with your body upright and make contact with how you are sitting: feet on the ground, bottom on the chair or cushion, body erect.

Calm the mind
Begin by taking three deep breaths.
Bring your attention in a friendly way to your breathing, observe the movement of breathing in and out and the gap between.
Bring your attention to the body, starting with attention for the sensations in the feet, legs, knees, hips, chest, arms, shoulders, back, neck, back of head, and face.
(longer silence)

15 Geoffrey W. Melville et al., "Fifteen minutes of chair-based yoga postures or guided meditation performed in the office can elicit a relaxations response," *Evidence-Based Complementary and Alternative Medicine* (2012).
16 In Holland, for example, Lizelotte Smits of the CNV, see: http://www.trouw.nl/tr/nl/4324/nieuws/article/detail/1792715/2010/09/15/Mediteren-is-een-gezond-tussendoortje.dhtml (visited on 16 May 2012 at 11:07 am).
17 Tan, *Search Inside Yourself* 149.

Failure

Now take four minutes to observe an experience of failure.

Bring your attention to a memory of an event in which you had the feeling of miserable failure: an aim you did not achieve, which disappointed yourself and others. Take the time to see, to hear, and to feel.

Observe the associated emotions and notice how they manifest themselves in the body.

(two minutes silence)

Then test whether you are capable of experiencing all those emotions without aversion.

See whether you can view the emotions you experience as physical sensations. That's all. They may be unpleasant, but they are only experiences. Allow these experiences simply to be present, to come as they will, and to go when they will. Let them be there, in a friendly, soft, generous way.

(longer silence)

Success

Then switch to spending four minutes on a more pleasurable experience, that of success.

Bring your attention to a memory of an event in which you had the feeling of considerable success: an aim you amply achieved, admired by everybody, in which you felt good about yourself. Take the time to see, to hear and to feel.

Observe the associated emotions and notice how they manifest themselves in the body.

(two minutes silence)

Then test whether you are capable of experiencing all those emotions without wanting to hang on to them.

See whether you can view the emotions you experience as physical sensations. That's all. They may be pleasant, but they are only experiences. Allow these experiences simply to be present, to come as they will, and to go when they will. Let them be there, in a friendly, soft, generous way.

(longer silence)

Back to the calmness
Then bring your attention back to the here and now, for about three minutes. Scan your body and observe how it now feels.
(silence)
Breathe in deeply and let go. Continue paying friendly attention to your breathing and, if it feels good for you, bring a hand to the chest and allow it to rest there.
(silence)
Continue observing what manifests itself in the body, then slowly open your eyes and close this meditation.

The effect of this meditation is that you can more easily cope with negative and positive experiences, without lapsing into aversion or wanting to keep them in your grasp. That increases your resilience, because you can react with greater awareness.

A less explicit way of keeping the resilience in your team up to scratch is consciously dealing with rest and silence in the team. With mindful teamwork, the manager ensures that the team members pause and take time to slow down a little, so that the drive for action is stopped for a moment. That is less difficult than is often thought. And there really is no need to spend hours meditating with your team. It begins with simple conversations over coffee or lunch. Reflect for a moment on an important contract has been won or on the treatment of a patient that is proving difficult. An awkward assignment that still has to be completed, but the deadline is frighteningly close. Take the time to celebrate successes together.

You can also do it by introducing short thinking pauses into meetings before a subject is discussed. In short, create moments to pause. We call that *slowing down to speed up* and it is at the heart of the green zone. It looks as though it costs time, but experience teaches that you can prove much more effective afterwards. We often have difficulty in taking time, exactly at the moment when we most need it. And that makes it so important that, as manager, you agree with your team that you will hold each other to this, that you may pause for a moment and listen to signals and experiences. That you give each other permission for this and not force each other to get on and live with it. Because that only weakens the resilience of the organization.

Using emotional intelligence

Once a certain robustness has been nurtured, space emerges for people to listen to each other and to see what is happening. Daniel Goleman has shown that using emotional intelligence is very good for mutual communication and collaboration.[18] Your role as manager is of considerable importance in this and that is because we, as people, are emotionally connected to our environment. Our moods and our emotional stability (and also our stress reactions) are constantly adjusted in relation to the moods and the emotions of others in our environment. Moods are *"contagious."* Negative emotions can hijack the mood. The result is that we listen less well to each other or recognize less well the other person's emotional condition. The group process is hampered. It can also work the other way round and, as manager, you play an important role in determining the mood in the group. Your mood sends the group in the right or wrong direction.

Emotional intelligence has four components. The first two – self-awareness and self-management – are personal competencies. You are aware of your own qualities, recognize your own inner experiences. And thus you are capable of managing yourself reasonably well; you understand your emotions, you take initiative, and you are generally optimistic. Together they form the foundation for the way you deal with people in your team and in your environment. On this foundation the other two components make their appearance: social awareness and management of relationships. Social awareness means understanding others in their emotions, fathoming the organization and what is happening in it, having feeling for what is necessary. And in your dealings with others, you can consciously influence, inspire, give direction, and solve conflicts.

18 Daniel Goleman, *Working with Emotional Intelligence* (New York: Bantam Books, 1998). Goleman describes emotional intelligence as: "the capacity for recognising our own feelings and those of others, for motivating ourselves, and for managing emotions well in ourselves and in our relationships."

To operate with emotional intelligence, you must, as manager, first and foremost be aware of your inner signals. Let us first look at how you can recognize your emotions and their impact.

Recognizing the impact of your emotions

For this exercise, you make use of a notebook. Decide that you will pause twice a day at a moment in which you, as leader, have emotional impact on your team. That can be in a conversation, a meeting, a conference, or during an informal gathering.

Start by making a note of what you observe in yourself: a thought, a physical sensation, a mood or emotion, an action. Perhaps you notice a combination of various elements. An example: you have just received an email saying that a certain report must be finished earlier and that you must ask your team to work a bit harder. For yourself, it means you will have to sacrifice a barbecue with your friends. Not a pleasant perspective. You're annoyed. And as you approach your team members, you notice that that feeling is still there. They look depressed as well. Your aversion grows...

But there's also another way: The same message, and you think it's a pity for that football evening. And then: how can I make the best of it? You know that your team members like some sort of reward: working late together but then first eating pizza together. You phone your secretary and get her to place an order. After saying you also think it's annoying, you make reference to a good experience you had of working together over a pizza. When you pass on the message, the team will react differently. You notice in yourself that the irritation is still there, but you also observe the pleasure of the prospect of getting to work together. You have already taken action. The group is hacked off, but you also see some happiness in their faces, because you have organized something.

You recognize emotions and their impact by naming the event and then paying attention to various aspects of the experience: physical sensations, thoughts, emotions, and the associated behavior. And you look at both your own experiences and the experiences that you observe in the reaction of the group: which sensations, thoughts, emotions, and behavior do you see in them?

Decide to make time every day to recognize the impact your emotions have on others.

In our trainings, we received surprising reactions:

"When I read through my notebook, I noticed that I had been down all week. And I also got somber reactions from my team."

"On Tuesday morning, I came to work in a really good mood after a delicious birthday breakfast. And even though we didn't have any time to celebrate my birthday, the mood remained good throughout the day."

"I can reasonably assess the mood in my team. Sometimes it feels heavy, and then I have the idea that they are in the pits. In the past, I would have gone along with them. Now I can regularly call out: hey guys, it really feels like the pits here. And then generally the laughter starts..."

What the experiences show is that mindfulness strengthens your ability to recognize emotions. In addition, it reveals the automatic reaction and that gives you the opportunity to influence the way emotions sweep you along. It helps not letting anger grow into an eruption, but see it coming in time. That prevents the eruption and you aren't swept along by an emotion. It creates space for a clear assessment or a consciously chosen measure. Recognizing your own emotions also helps with empathy, feeling how another feels. And that makes relationship management easier.

It becomes a bit more difficult when you apply recognizing the impact to awkward situations. For example, when there is a difference of opinion, a style of communication you don't really like, a person whose power, role, cultural background is not yours, or if a major change in the organization is proposed. It is exactly in such situations that our emotions are easily activated, and the fight or flight reaction is triggered in our body. In such a situation, when differences are concerned, it is worth taking a look at the language in which they are expressed. Which images and metaphors are evoked? And how are the differences dealt with? Are they – politely

– waved aside with a "that doesn't matter, we are all equal" or are they welcomed as a possibility for creativity?

Recognizing reactions to awkward situations[19]

Take time to wander around your workplace and observe how your team members react physically and emotionally to awkward situations such as differences of opinion, differences in dominant position, sex or cultural background, differences in style of communications etc.

Observe what sort of awkward situation it is. Observe what sort of language is used and the variations in facial expressions (such as blushing, pulling faces, turning white, etc.). Notice in particular whether you observe a hardening, rigidity or a withdrawal movement – a small movement, such as slightly tightening the jaw, a light coloring of the skin – followed by a recovery or an attempt at "managing" the reaction.

Observe how you react yourself to an awkward situation, in particular one that is not especially welcome. Where do you tighten, mentally or physically?

Which parts of your body contract, ready to flee or to fight?

Which parts of your body come into action to fight? Or retract and pull back, ready to flee?

How and where do you freeze, caught in the area between fleeing and fighting, tossed back and forth between the two?

Complete the exercise by making notes in your notebook. What strikes you, what is new for you?

The experiences with this exercise are rather confrontational, because we are not accustomed to acknowledging our physical reactions to differences. A few examples:

---

19 Amanda Ridings, *Pause for Breath* (London: Live it Publishing, 2011). 137.

"I hardly dare mention it, but I thought her reaction so excessive, with that high toneless little voice. I couldn't do anything with it. Had the inclination to shut her up."

"When the boss said that the team would be reorganized, I turned ice cold. I wanted to crawl under the table. When he had finished with his long-winded story, I was hot and had turned red, ready to punch him in the face."

"There they were, arguing again. I immediately walked off in the other direction. Let them sort it out."

When things become tense, our reaction becomes stronger. That is what these examples teach us and that easily leads to an uncomfortable mood and avoidance behavior in your team. A trigger and at the same time a strong reaction. How can you avoid that? The following exercise helps you cope with it.

Coping with awkward emotions[20]

If you do this exercise in a group, it is handy to split the group up into small groups of three. Each of the three gets two minutes to talk (the others listen with full attention without asking questions or speaking) about a situation in which they were triggered to a negative emotion or reaction.

Directing attention
Begin by taking three deep breaths.
Bring your attention to your breathing, observe the movement of breathing in and out and the gaps between.

Negative emotion
Shift the attention for two minutes to the negative emotion.
Allow a memory of an unpleasant event to surface, an experience of frustration, anger, hurt, or an experience in which you were triggered.
See whether you can mentally live through that experience again, with all the associated emotions.

20 Tan, *Search Inside Yourself:* 118.

Coping with negative emotions

The following step is to practice our response for seven minutes.

The first two steps are stopping and breathing. Stopping at the start of a trigger is an important pause. You can strengthen it by directing the mind to the breathing and not reacting to the emotion. If you like, you can breathe deeply and slowly. And remain in the pause condition for around thirty seconds.

(30 seconds of silence)

The following step is observing. We do that by experiencing the emotion in our body. Bring your attention to the body. How does an oppressive emotion feel in your body? In your face? In your neck, your shoulders, your chest, your back? Also observe the differences in temperature and in tension.

Experience it without judgment. At this point it is important to experience the emotional difficulty as simply a physical phenomenon and not as an existential phenomenon. The experience is not "I am angry", but: "I experience anger in my body."

Take a minute to experience the physiology of the emotion in the body.

(one minute silence)

Next, we reflect.

Where does the emotion come from? Is there a history attached to it? If this experience concerns another person, place yourself in his or her shoes and look at yourself. Recall this statement in your mind: "Everybody wants to be happy. This person thinks that this way of acting will make him happy, in one way or another." Put it into perspective, without judging whether it is right or wrong.

(30 seconds of silence)

Then we react.

Look at ways in which you can react to this situation and which positive consequences that would have. You do not have to do it – just imagine for yourself how you would be able to give a very friendly, positive reaction. What would that look like? Take the coming minute to prepare that response.

(one minute silence)

Back to the here and now

And return again to the here and now. Take two minutes for this.
Bring your attention to the breathing.

(short silence)

Clench your fist firmly and hold the remaining emotion in it. Slowly open your fingers and allow the energy to flow away.

Bring your attention back to your body as a whole, your breathing
or wherever your mind experiences the greatest stability. Keep your
attention there for the rest of the time.

Managing emotions in your team

Recognizing your emotions and learning to cope with the awkward edges of them makes you better capable of playing your
role as manager in your team. For you must naturally also learn
to handle the emotions of people in your team. An example: last
year I was accompanying a team as organizational consultant to
a retreat in the country. Just as we were about to begin, one of the
members ran in. He was full of irritation about the place and
time, which had caused him a lot of problems and he was late because he had had to take his children to school and then got stuck
in traffic. It was, apparently, all a bit too much for him. In a calm
tone I said that I could understand that discomfort and his irritation and that I was pleased he had been able to get here so quickly. The effect of recognizing his irritation was that it quickly subsided.

And that is exactly how you, as manager, can show that emotions are allowed in the green zone of mindfulness, without them
hijacking us. Having attention for the emotional undercurrents
of individuals and of the group as a whole. You have two options
for this: act as a manager who wants to keep the lid on everything
(perhaps because you find it awkward yourself) or view your role
as the person who sees them and encourages others to cope better with them. The lid-on-things manager has fixed convictions
about right and wrong. Employees who do not satisfy the standard are pitiful. What happens is that the manager masks his uncertainties and vulnerabilities behind a sort of superiority. Naturally you don't want that, but it is striking how easily we adopt

smaller forms of that: the other is just a little less smart, handy or thorough than yourself, isn't he?

Red light emotions	Green light emotions	Amber light emotions
Nature:	Nature:	Nature:
• Frozen thinking • Tension in body • Focus on past and future • Winning-losing • Me first • Causing damage	• Open and flexible • Synchronous with body • In the now • Provided for relationship need • Makes vulnerability surface • Us first • Helping	• Arise when things go differently than thought • Feel anxious in the body • Triggered when unrealistic expectations cannot be achieved or when a barrier appears in conversation
Aggression	Alarm	Frustration
Gloominess	Sadness	Disappointment
Yearning	Love/appreciation	Emotional yearning
Anxiety	Empathy	Fear
Venomous/sigh	Joy	Shyness
Jealousy	Compassion	Guilt
Contempt	Admiration	Insult

The encouraging manager ensures open communication about feelings and emotions. He or she views them as signals of what is happening and tries to ascertain where they come from and what they mean. A team member's anger can be a signal that something is happening. As manager, you do not react to this by stopping it or rejecting it, but with investigative openness. In this way, you create attention for the emotional undercurrent, you create an environment in which they are welcome.

A handy aid for learning to cope with the impact of emotions is to divide them into a few categories. Some emotions are by nature more open, others more closed, and others are somewhere in between. They can be compared to the colors of a traffic light. If you recognize the types, you can cope with them more easily.

For you, as manager, the amber light emotions are the most interesting to work with. Often anger and vulnerability are behind them and they are accompanied by a certain defensive attitude in your employee. By being open and welcoming, you can ensure that employees can express themselves and are able to study their feeling. In this way, you make it possible for them to remain attached to the group.

From that attention, they take responsibility for sensing each other well and being alert to what everybody is experiencing. In a planning session at a technology company, everything actually went according to the familiar patterns. The board had set a challenging objective for next year, as they always did. The group topped that with bravura: we'll go for double figures! But there was one team member who felt a little uncomfortable with this careless way of setting objectives, because the reality was that production was running a long way behind. He felt embarrassed, but at the invitation of the manager, who saw him sitting there rather withdrawn, he gathered his courage and said: "Are you really ready to do that? Let's go for 400% growth. Then we'll be serious!" The group looked at him, a respected team member, with amazement. Had he gone crazy? Until, after a few seconds, a smile appeared on his face. He had provoked them into making good on their promises and had pointed out a hidden group norm, namely making empty claims. And this led to an open discussion about what really mattered.

With an encouraging attitude, you can make use of the emotions in your team. That doesn't always have to be in words and very intentional and clever; it can often be a simple gesture or glance. But by pausing at emotions, you set a norm: we are all in the same boat, everybody belongs. And that in turn lays the basis for paying attention in conversations to everybody's perspective, even that of the troublemakers or the quiet ones in the group. Or to attention for the difficulty that certain jobs or learning processes involve. In this way, an emotionally intelligent team develops open communications.

A culture of dialogue

Now that you have learned to direct the resilience and emotional intelligence of your team, we will, in this paragraph, look at how to build on this and use mindfulness in team communication. Mindfulness means that you can switch more smartly between action and reflection and thus better cope with that on which you direct your attention. And directing your attention is exactly what communication is all about: with whom do I communicate and in which way, how do I approach the other person and do I thereby allow myself to be carried away in my own emotions and fixed mindset or do I have the resilience to work with an open mindset? As manager, this is how you set to work to establish a dialogue culture in your team.

Below I will deal with various forms of communication that belong in the toolbox of the mindful manager and his team, alternated with practical exercises. Starting with the basic forms of listening with or without completely open attention. Then methods for mindful conversing with each other, or rather: entering into a dialogue. I will end with mindful meetings.

Listening with attention

Mindful communication starts with listening well. And you can do that in various ways. Forms of listening that are appropriate to a more open or closed mindset, directed more from the part or from the whole. In line with Scharmer, I distinguish four forms of listening that are summarized in the table below.[21] Each form has its own way of paying attention. The first two are forms that you encounter with the autopilot, because your world view and all suppositions are fixed in this. The third and fourth better match the conscious response, whereby you react to a situation with increasing openness. Immediately after the summary you will find an exercise for learning to distinguish the four forms during a dialogue walk.

---

21 C. Otto Scharmer, *Theorie U. Leiding vanuit de toekomst die zich aandient* (Zeist: Christofoor, 2010). From 321.

Form of listening	Type of attention	Characterizing
Downloading	From yourself as the center; fixed world view	You can compare this to "in one ear and out the other." You only need half a word to know what you must do, or to confirm to yourself how the other is. A form of listening that we daily apply very practically, the autopilot.
Factual listening	From the edge of you own world view without affecting it	This form of listening is directed mainly at noticing differences: in facts, in arguments, in word use, in images. An undertone of "this is wrong" or "this is different from what I wanted or what it should have been." A useful form of listening that is frequently used in legal environments, by lawyers, for example.
Empathic listening	From the position of the other; you leave your own world view	Here the listener tries to imagine how something feels for the other, shifting into his or her situation. It is not your own experience or attentiveness that is central, but the experience of the other.
Generative listening	From what is going to come, without world view	Listening between the lines is what you could call this. Discovering the story behind the story. With

> this type of listening there is the most room for creativity, for new possibilities arising. I sometimes compare it to the moment that you are in the shower and suddenly think "Oh yes, now I get it. That's the solution!"

The dialogue walk: learning to know forms of listening

Reserve around half an hour for this exercise. Take a walk with a colleague, during which one speaks and the other listens. The speaker may talk freely about whatever is concerning him. And if there is nothing to say, then a period of silence is just fine. There is no obligation to speak. Say whatever occurs to you, without reticence. You have fifteen minutes, all for yourself. You can talk about an issue that is concerning you in your role as manager or about something in your private life. How to deal with a certain issue, for example, or with an employee.

The listener walks next to you and pays you his full attention. But he or she does not react, doesn't hum, doesn't ask questions. He or she is just there. Here and now. During the walk, the listener keeps tabs on the time.

After fifteen minutes, you exchange roles. The speaker becomes listener and the listener speaker.

When both have had their turn, you finish the exercise. If you like, you can write down your experiences during the listening in a notebook.

When doing this exercise in a group, I always first ask about the experiences of the listener. What was it like listening in that way, without interrupting? And then I ask the speaker: what was it like to be able to speak freely.

The various experiences reveal the stratification of the four forms of listening and the differences in type of attention.

Most participants who do this exercise are confronted with our daily conventions and habits in speaking and listening. After all, we have in our culture all sorts of standards of politeness about how we converse with each other. And then insight into the various forms of listening is gained.

> *"Goodness, I felt so uncomfortable, so impolite not to show how I was empathizing with the other. That's not for me!"*
>
> *"I really had to restrain myself. Constantly had the urge to ask a question or to say that I had experienced something similar."*
>
> *"Every time she told me something, a whole train of thought ran through my mind: that I would have done it differently; stupid to do it like that; but didn't you see that coming. All judgments... I had difficulty stopping the stream."*
>
> *"What I noticed after a while was that his story took on a different tone. First it was very factual. Then it became more sensitive, more vulnerable. There were emotions."*
>
> *"At the start, I had the idea that she was rationalizing toward solutions. In the course of the conversation, things changed. Then suddenly it was about her father and mother and the role they had played in her life."*
>
> *"When I was talking about it, I had the feeling as if I were swimming, as if there was no firm ground beneath my feet because the other didn't react. Oddly enough, I didn't feel all alone, but it was a strange experience."*
>
> *"It was wonderful to be able to talk so freely and not be interrupted. I had the idea that I could follow my own way in the story. That really helped me move on."*
>
> *"That space to talk is fine, you are not forced into the other's framework. For me, that gave me a feeling of space for myself and also space for creativity."*

Once you have experienced the differences between the various forms of listening and paying attention, it is handy to take a look at them at work. You can train yourself as manager to be aware of which listening form you use and when you switch from one to the other. For routine conversations, downloading will sometimes be enough, but if you really want to set to work on coaching or steering your employees, an empathic or generative form is much more useful. And so you learn from mindfulness to switch your attention between various forms of listening.

Listening forms at work

In order to take a look at your own listening mode at work – again making use of a notebook – take time throughout a whole week to note how you are listening at various moments. Are you "downloading" or listening factually? Empathic or generative?
Observe your listening mode during conversations or meetings. Can you switch the mode? Which moments are you in one mode and which in the other? What causes that? Your mood? The other person? The situation?
Make notes for a week and take a look at your listening modes. What does that teach you?

A few experiences:

"I noticed that in the afternoon I was more frequently in the habit listening mode than in the morning. Apparently I shut myself off more when I'm tired."
"If a conversation with an employee appears to be tense, I am more quickly in the differentiating listening mode. I catch myself wanting to be proved right or to convince him. Sometimes I have to take a deep breath, and give myself the space to listen properly again. That also changes the mood of the conversation."
"Last week, two employees came to me with a problem. I didn't have an immediate solution. I sat down and asked questions. At a certain moment I thought, maybe that's the solution. It just popped up between the lines. None of us had thought of it before, but it worked."

The powerful effect of listening well is that you develop an open mind and that has several qualities. It starts with the recognition that what we think is a construct of our mind. We also call that an artifact, something that is made, whether by ourselves or by others. It is nothing definite. You could compare it to a photo or a drawing; those are also made. Some things are shown in a cer-

tain color or shape, others are not; it is a selection and an interpretation. And the same is true of our thinking, with the idea that
we have of a certain situation or person. It is exactly this conclusion that makes it possible to let go of an idea and to realize that
we can think differently. Development, evolution, adaptation,
and innovation are possible if we let go of what we have learned.
An open mindset goes in search of creativity, allows space for it.
Even dares to start with a new, empty canvas, just like a painter.
An open minded mindset dares not to know, to sit still quietly
and observe what happens. And enters into the dialogue from
not knowing, dares to hold up the self-evident to discussion, to
discover what there is and what is possible.[22]

Ladder of Inference

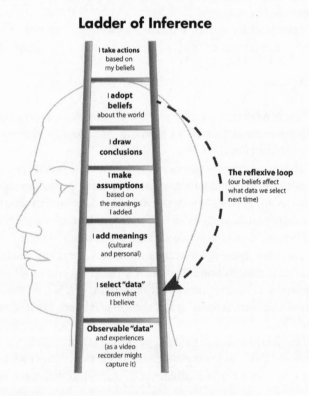

22 For an inspiring description of the open mind: Edel Maex, *Open Mind.*
Anders kijken naar de werkelijkheid (Gent: Witsand Uitgevers, 2009).

Now that you have developed various forms of listening with attention as manager with your team, you can now take the next step towards communicating. You hold a conversation, a discussion. Management of your team or setting to work together as team means communicating. And then the first thing you encounter is the autopilot, now in the guise of the ladder of inference. This works quickly and convincingly, for within a few seconds we draw conclusions based on observations (or a selection of observations) linked to convictions (generally already existing). The ladder is a wonderful (I think) illustration of the defense mechanism that is present in every team against seeing the situation for what it is. It leads to a restrictive reaction, instead of an open one.[23] You are in doing mode and rapidly climb the ladder. With mindfulness, you can teach your team to descend the ladder again in being mode.

An example from my own practice as a management consultant. Toward the end of my presentation of a project design for a change process, I see Peter slouching at the end of the table. He hasn't asked any questions and I don't really know what to make of him. That he is slouching is not a sign of interest, I suddenly think. In the interview I had with him, he wasn't really that responsive. Then he sits up and asks the chairman: "Could he write down everything in a report? I think we should take time to study the proposal." Just when I had expected a go-ahead, he throws a spanner in the works. Inside, I am boiling with rage and the thought passes through me that in any case I won't be including his material in my report. What a pity that he is the deputy director of the department... I forget to ask what he meant.

I could of course have done that. An open question such as: "Peter, what is your reaction now that you've heard my story?" or "Am I right in thinking that my story is boring you?" could have helped. Then I wouldn't have scaled the ladder and perhaps I would have stopped at the first or second rung.

23 Chris Argyris, *Overcoming Organizational Defenses* (Upper Saddle River New Jersey: Prentice Hall, 1990). Peter Senge, *De vijfde discipline* (Schiedam: Scriptum, 1992).

To prevent this scaling of the ladder and thus to strengthen the communicative skills of both yourself and your team, you need a better quality of conversation and dialogue, in which you make better use of your attention. We do that with mindful dialogue, the principles of which were developed by the American meditation teacher, Gregory Kramer.[24] The core of this is to use an important skill in exercising mindfulness during communication: the skill of stopping doing. You stop the autopilot during communication and thus escape from the conditioning of the mind that holds you in its grasp as soon as you scale the ladder.

You will have noticed by the listening exercise described above that as soon as you open your mouth, the mindfulness seems to fly away and mindlessness takes its place. The head takes over, the attention is dragged along with it. You are dragged along in your own story, that of the other person, and in jumping around in exchanges with each other. Sensory experiences, the presence in the combination of body and mind evaporate. Feedback signals are no longer picked up. Then pausing, stopping for a moment is required. To escape from the autopilot in communicating. Stop for a moment in your "mental run." By realizing that you are present in the here and now, in this moment, in this body, in this conversation or this meeting.

The mindful dialogue

For this exercise, you need three people. Two participants in the dialogue exercise, the third as time keeper.

You sit down comfortably next to each other in a chair or on cushions. Next to each other but facing in opposite directions, so the right side is next to the right side of the person sitting next to you. You do not need to look at each other during this exercise and you listen with the full attention of all your senses.

Next, one speaks and the other listens. The listener listens, but does not react.

The speaker tells something in response to a question. For example: "What is happening at the moment in your role as manager?" After

24 Gregory Kramer, *Insight Dialogue* (Boston: Shambhala, 2007).

a number of minutes, the time keeper rings a bell. The speaker stops. After a minute, the bell sounds again and the speaker continues speaking but not necessarily continuing the story. After stopping, a moment of relaxation follows. The speaker feels the stomach, the breath, the feet, the body. Space may enter the feeling. And then the speaker continues with what at that moment presents itself to him or her as the story. Perhaps a different story, a new perspective, a deeper layer in the story. Whatever it is. There is no obligation for consistency.

And so speaking and being silent alternate, four or five times.

Then the turn passes to the next, until both have had a go.

The core of the exercise consists of the following steps:[25]

Pause

If we pause, we step out of the pressure of conditioned thoughts and feelings, and this naturally leads to awareness. If you no longer feed the stream of thoughts and feelings through identification, mindfulness is the natural result. Pausing is delaying, you bring space between what you hear, see, and think, and what you say. We can really absorb what is being said, how we feel and the color of this moment. We become aware of our body and feelings. We step out of the reaction that normally takes over, whether that is negative (fear, irritation, anger etc.), or positive (excitement, joy).

Relax

Naturally we cannot relax our body by issuing an order, we cannot stop thinking on command. Relaxation means being present at the experience, stop fighting the experience. We meet the experience with acceptance. Perhaps we can relax areas in our body and we bring acceptance to whatever remains tense. Relaxation means accepting things as they are, whether it is about pain, injured feelings, joy or rejection.

25 Ibid., from 107.

Open
Then we open ourselves, expand our internal experience further from the "me," [...] opening ourselves to the other means that we do not have a certain agenda, do not wish to fulfill a task, do not want to make a point or develop a plan. We only come into this moment to see what is going to happen.

Trust what emerges
Everything that happens in mindful dialogue are natural processes, not aims. Just as with the walking meditation, we see how the moment unfolds. We trust that the good things, the wisdom of open communication in the contact, will display themselves the more we develop an open perception. The directive "trust what emerges" brings us to experiencing what it is like to be alone with another person, or a group of people, in the present moment, not looking ahead to what will happen in the future.

Intense listening
During the listening, you can discover different layers to what is being said. The content of what is being said, unusual words and phrases. Observe the significance that develops in the mind. Then shift your attention to emotions. And to the reactions that that causes in your body. Which tone of speaking do you observe? Notice how you sometimes listen with focus and then with a sort of broad openness.

Speak the truth
You will discover that, in this way, you will speak with greater awareness. The truth of the experience of this moment. And there too you can recognize different layers. They have one thing in common. People speak at the right moment, with cordiality, with good will.

The insightful dialogue is a basic form of open and connecting communication, in which the autopilot is stopped and, by stopping the mental running, space is made for creative solutions and actions. Experiences of participants in the training:

"Surprising how much depth there is in a conversation. At least I do not feel pressured into giving an immediate answer."
"As listener, I saw the creative moments bubbling up in the other almost by themselves. Yet at first I thought I would have to help her."
"After a while, I feel capable of having so much attention for what the other is saying as for my own experiences. Almost simultaneously."

With this skill you are, as manager, much better capable of holding conversations with your employees or keeping an eye on your own reactions during conversations with your employees and then choosing a conscious response. You learn to keep your attention on both your own experiences and those of your conversation partner – a rapid switching process.

As manager, you can find the practical translation of the attentive dialogue skill in the application of the communication forms *advocacy* and *inquiry*.[26] In conversations with your team mates or with colleague managers, you must regularly put forward your standpoint in order to ensure that it is heard or that a policy decision turns out differently than proposed. Then use of your attention is extraordinarily useful. During your argument, you not only have attention for the others but also for your own reactions – and then there is balance. And then you can increase the quality with which you argue your standpoint. The same thing applies if you sit in a meeting where somebody else argues a case or when you are in a conversation with an employee. By carefully directing your attention, you can make better use of inquiring questions and you prevent yourself being satisfied too quickly with what is said, or that you scale the ladder yourself. The skill of being able to hold mindful dialogue means that you communicate better in your role as manager.

26 Derived from: Senge, *De noodzakelijke revolutie:* from 249.

Advocacy and inquiry

Advocacy		Inquiry	
Make your own thought process transparent while you scale the ladder		*Ask others to make their thought process transparent and help them descend the ladder*	
What you do	What you say	What you do	What you say
• Formulate your assumptions and describe how you reached them. Explain your assumptions.	• This is what I think and this is why.	• Lead people along the ladder and investigate their assumptions	• What brings you to this conclusion? Which data do you have for this? What drives you to say that?
• Explain the implications of your viewpoint. Who is affected? How and why?	• I assume that...	• Do not use aggressive language.	• Not: what do you mean? but: can you help me understand your line of thought?
• Try during speaking to imagine how other people hear what you say.	• In order to get a good picture, you can imagine that you are a customer who will be affected...	• Try to fathom why they say something	• What is its significance? How is this connected with your other concerns?
• Provoke questions to assess your assumptions and conclusions.	• What do you think of what I just claimed? Are there weak points in my reasoning?	• Explain why you pose a question.	• I ask you that because I...
• Don't be defensive, and indicate where your thinking is not yet clear.	• One point in particular about which I would like feedback...	• Ask for a broader context.	• How would you influence the proposal ...? Is that the same as...? Can you give a typical example?
		• Ensure that you understand what the others have said.	• Am I right that you are saying that...?

Listen, remain open, and encourage others to put forward deviating opinions.	_Listen to whether you understand something in a new way. Do not concentrate on your own agenda or rebutting other people's reasons._

You can use your skill in advocacy and inquiry to communicate better with your team in meetings. I am not telling you anything new if I once again remind you that communication studies show that the major part of our communication is non-verbal. 55% of communication is through our body language and 38% through the tone of our voice. That explains the importance of emotional intelligence. And only 7% of our communication is verbal. The way in which you sit in a meeting and the way in which you communicate can be of vital importance. The core here is how you are present and whether you can listen well and notice what actually takes place. So that you do not hold the meeting on autopilot and you and your team can give conscious replies to the questions and subjects dealt with. Below are a number of tips for mindful meetings.

Mindful meetings
Meetings are often a continuation of our mental running. With the attitude of "the quicker we're done with it the better. Then I can get back to real work." But it is exactly that mental running, the haste that arises, that causes us to be less than relaxed in the meeting and because of that the conversation runs less effectively and rapidly than we had wanted.
There are a number of steps for holding meetings more mindfully:

The transition to the meeting
To start with, it is handy to take some time before you go to a meeting. Let go for a moment the tasks you are doing and take, for example, a short breathing space. You can also take the time to realize how you normally go to the meeting and allow yourself this time to be more relaxed.
Certainly, if you are the chairman, it is good to go to the meeting

attentively. What do you notice in yourself: physical sensations, thoughts, emotions?

Arriving at the meeting
When you enter the meeting room, take time for it. Feel how you sit, listen to your breathing. Also absorb your surroundings. You are now here. Look around, observe how your colleagues are sitting. Their clothing, their poise, you can even greet them inside yourself with a friendly smile.

Remain observant
During the meeting, you play the game of observing. Observe in yourself how you react when somebody says something. Observe also the thoughts – sometimes judgmental – about what others say. And then simply try to absorb what they say, both verbally and non-verbally, in you. Do you hear the tone of voice? Do you see their body language?
Also notice how often or how quickly you want to intervene, or when you actually want to withdraw from the conversation. See what it's like if you nevertheless continue.

Join in
And join in the conversation. By asking questions. By putting forward your arguments. Each time noticing what happens with you. Without having to score points.

By introducing a culture of dialogue, you provide communicative substance as manager to the green zone of mindfulness in your team: you listen deeply (with an eye and ear open to emotions) and react lucidly and consciously with an open mind, and you tackle the dialogue and communicate openly in conversations by – in the background – using insightful dialogue and to deal consciously with meetings. You thus show how you can consciously direct the attention of yourself and your team at what is necessary.

Compassionate performance

In a team, you work together on achieving results. The way towards that and the way in which you do it matter. With the green zone of mindfulness you can do it in a conscious way, whereby the autopilot and mechanisms that obstruct change are stopped by resilience, emotional intelligence, and a culture of dialogue. But it is still about performing and achieving results. And the last component of the green zone is how you can deliver an important contribution to the success of your team by using compassionate performing.

Compassion is sometimes described as "empathy in action." To be empathetic and to be able to place yourself in the feelings of colleagues, you must, just as with mindfulness, postpone your judgment and deploy your curiosity toward people and their experiences. Naturally we can never be completely without judgment, for we need a certain grip, but postponing is essential for curiosity towards the other. Look, connect, and see what they need.[27] And then come into action.

Previously, I wrote that successful teams take joint responsibility for the intended results and for each other, for the mutual collaboration. Both elements are found again in compassionate performing: honesty about the course of events *and* undertaking the job together form joint responsibility.

And that is exactly what compassion is all about: feeling involved in the discomfort or the pain of others combined with the desire and the action to do something about it.

In order to correct the idea that compassion is something very soft, I will offer an example that clearly shows it can be highly practical.[28] The first example is about Tom, the managing partner of a large law firm, who notices that invoicing is very low on the priority list of the lawyers. As COO, he is responsible for finances, IT, and HR, but how do you get such a subject high on the list of pri-

27 Richard Boyatzis and Annie McKee, *Resonant Leadership* (Cambridge: Harvard Business Press, 2005). 179-80.
28 Examples derived from: ibid., Chapter 8. Compassion.

orities of a group that is headstrong, performance-driven, and independent? His advantage is that he is a lawyer and understands how the others think and feel. He knows the pressure they are under and the frustrations and passions they have. So he knows that simply issuing an order will not work. And using that empathy, he came up with a different solution, one that suited the group of people he was dealing with. And with which he could, as authority, ensure that they really wanted what he asked of them. His solution was simple and effective. He organized the group into teams which had to ensure invoices were sent out and payments were made. They were given objectives. And around this he organized an open invoice submission and payment collection competition to reward the fastest submitter and collector, with prizes such as umbrellas, polo shirts, and vouchers for restaurants and movies, and yes, even money. The lawyers became completely addicted to this game and writing invoices and collecting payments became an important priority. It worked because he connected with their affinity for friendly competition (it wasn't about the money) and openly winning or losing (they liked that), but the losers were not punished (that would have created a negative overtone). The tone of performance remained compassionate, working together, and no punishments.

Compassion has a positive effect, because it appeals to the mental, emotional, and physical health and so contributes to the results of or the mood in the team.[29] The importance of compassion is again underlined because we are much more dependent on teamwork, both for individual performance and for our ambitions as a whole. If we work across organizational borders, that is even stronger. We cannot get any further without each other. Below I give an exercise with which you can strengthen your own compassion by increasing your friendliness for others.

29 Ibid., 185.

Multiplying friendliness
Calm the mind
To start with, bring your attention for a few minutes to your breathing.

Multiply your friendliness
Then make contact with the good sides in yourself: your love, compassion, altruism, and inner joy. If you like, you can visualize that goodness as a beam of rays emitted by your body.
(short silence)
As you breathe in, you breathe all your goodness into your heart. Use your heart to multiply your goodness by a factor of ten. And as you breathe out, send all that goodness into the whole world. If you like, you can visualize this as a beam of rays.
(two minutes silence)
Then make contact with the goodness of everybody you know. Everybody is a good person and has something good. If you like, you can also visualize their goodness as a beam of rays. As you breathe in, you breathe all their goodness toward your heart...
Repeat this step.
(two minutes silence)
And finally make contact with the goodness of all the inhabitants of the world. Everybody has at least something good. And again you can visualize this as you wish. Breathe in the goodness toward your heart.
Repeat this step.
(two minutes silence)

Closure
End the exercise with a short period of attention for your breathing.

Participants at our trainings often feel some embarrassment when they do this exercise for the first time.

> *"Gee, I was glad I had my eyes closed. It's rather embarrassing to think about so much goodness. Is it really necessary?"*
> *"About half way through the exercise, I began to feel somewhat easier, somewhat softer. It's actually rather funny to pause at*

goodness. I realize how often we are hard to each other."
"All at once, I had to smile. I thought of Peter. Yesterday, I was an-
gry at him all day. I reminded myself how he had helped me the
day before."

But after the embarrassment there comes the realization of friendliness, toward others, and toward ourselves. It makes it easier to
discuss or change things among ourselves; the involvement with
others becomes greater.

Ed Schein, the American specialist in organizational culture and
change, says that learning to accept help from each other and giving it to each other is crucial for teamwork. According to him, it is
just as essential for teams in normal organizations as for teams
who carry out open heart surgery. The heart surgeon, the anesthe-
tist, the perfusionist, and the nurses are directly dependent on
each other in the here and now. There, everybody helps, not as a
result of authority but because it is necessary. Each person has his
or her share in the result. The nurse will call out "stop doctor"
without any hesitation if he picks up the wrong instrument and
thus offers support and help.

The organization of such teamwork requires the green zone of
mindfulness. Schein calls it "cultural islands" where people step
over the hierarchy of their position and enter into a genuine personal relationship with each other. In the heart surgery team, the
surgeon must relinquish his hierarchical position and operate on an
equal footing with the nurse. And the reverse is also necessary for
the success of the team: the nurse must not act as a subservient if a
crucial mistake seems about to be made. In the green zone, you explicitly enter into a mutual helping relationship.[30] The mindful
team-check-in can help in this and I describe it below in an actual
example.

30 Art Kleiner and Rutger von Post, "A Corporate Climate of Mutual Help,"
   Strategy + Business, no. 62 (2011). And also: Edgar H. Schein, *Helping* (San
   Francisco: Berrett-Koehler, 2009).

Mindful team-check-in

In Columbus, Ohio in the United States, a gynecologist uses the mindful check-in in the operating theater, in order to create the shared intention for compassionate collaboration for the benefit of the patient. After running through the mandatory checklists, he does a human check-in. He introduces the patient, tells something about her background in order to humanize the person behind the patient. And then he explains what they are going to do to help her and why. Next, he has everybody assisting check-in, who they are, and what their role is, and what their intention is to be as helpful as possible to achieve a successful outcome of the surgery. They only begin to operate when everybody has focused his or her full attention on what they are doing and who they are doing it for.[31]

Why not try this check-in, in the weekly team meeting, or if you and your team are on the eve of an important action or project. And really take the time for it, for the factual matters, but also for feelings, emotions, and intentions of your team members.

In the meantime, all sorts of studies have shown that compassion in teams is useful. In a software company where a team of employees meditated on friendliness and compassion there was a clearly perceptible effect on the positive content of their emotions, their perception of life, future and mutual support, while somber thoughts and feelings declined.[32] Their performance was noticeably better, and so too was the mood at work. Another study shows that greater self-compassion makes people better resistant to negative events (it increases the resilience!) and enables them to take greater personal initiative and acquire greater skill in dealing with awkward issues. They are less afraid of making mistakes and admitting them, because they have more self-respect and can look at their own deficiencies with sympathy. They display more emotional intelligence and approach emotions, even difficult ones, with friendliness instead of rejection.

---

31 With thanks to Phil Cass, CEO of Columbus Medical Association and Affiliates who told me this example.

32 Erik van den Brink and Frits Koster, *Compassievol leven. Van mindfulness naar heartfulness* (Amsterdam: Boom, 2012). 78.

And they have greater social connectedness.[33] Exactly the things that belong in the green zone.

Compassion in teamwork does not only support mutual involvement, but also mutual honestly. It introduces the quality based on mindfulness of having the courage to view things honestly. I call that unconditional honesty. That honesty is not so easy. Perhaps you have to recognize that you had too high expectations for the results or that you encountered unexpected obstacles during the execution in the mutual collaboration. We sometimes prefer to avoid viewing things critically and sharply, because we don't really want to deal with individual faults. Admitting that something has gone wrong through your actions or giving commentary on the behavior of a colleague is not simple. But it is necessary, in order to prevent accidents happening or to avoid major damage. Or to learn from it. You should not underestimate its importance: I previously referred to the study that shows that surgical teams function better if they report more mistakes! Mindfulness promotes openness and honesty, inducing a greater awareness in people that they do not wish to make any violation of their ethical standards, the study shows. They want to fulfill those principles and not just show them. One study shows that to achieve this it is important that managers invite employees to pause for a moment at their experiences before they say something or take decisions.[34]

Unrelenting honesty means going back to what the ambition or desired result was, to the task that had to be done and the way in which it was pursued. Teams regularly become frustrated; the discussions are dull and nobody really wants to talk about it, helplessness rules, there is cynicism and distrust. You then see such a team escape in beautiful prospects about new products and services or choose the easy solution of replacing a team member or the manager or have an external team building session. We must cooperate better, is the often-used panacea. But then there has been no unre-

34 Ruedy and Schweitzer, "In the Moment: The Effect of Mindfulness on Ethical Decision Making," 81-82.

lenting review of what it was all about or how it arose. Only by acknowledging the actual reality of the assignment or task is it possible to state what is the matter. Only then can experiences be given a place, and only then can you start learning from them. You can do this with your team using the following exercise.

Mindful evaluating and learning

Take enough time for a mindful evaluation and learning exercise. Depending on the action involved, at least an hour, preferably two. Begin the evaluation with a period of silence, for example five minutes, in which you ask everybody to bring their attention to their breathing and in which you direct your attention to all senses (taste, touch, sight, hearing, smell). This helps sharpen the memory of the project or activity.

Then you ask all participants to pause in their minds for a short while on the honesty and courage to bring up things. And invite them to do just that.

Then you ask all participants to imagine the action, with as many sensory perspectives as possible.

Then ask all participants to write down all aspects they have noticed, both comfortable and less comfortable ones, in their notebook. Take around ten minutes for that.

Then you begin mutual exchange, in which everybody shares their notes, based on the following questions:

1. What did we want to do?
2. What actually happened?
3. Why did it happen?
4. What are we going to do next time?

You can best ask each other open questions about all comments in order to clarify matters. And then summarize the main lines and extract the points that must be studied further or about which agreements can already be made.

Next, you do a second round, in which you delve deeper into what you can learn. For this you can use the following questions:

1. What was the greatest success in our approach from which we can learn?
2. What were the greatest difficulties we encountered and how did we overcome them?
3. Which additions or changes must we implement in our approach and what must be excluded?
4. Which matters were not solved satisfactorily and require attention? Based on what you have learned, what is your recommendation?

End this round after a mutual dialogue by summarizing conclusions and, where necessary, make agreements for follow up.[35]

Using this honesty, you can, as manager, ensure that no hard judgmental performance culture arises in your team, but that you work with honest feedback, in which the starting point is that you constantly care for and help each other. The summary below clearly shows the difference between both forms of feedback.

Judge or learn from each other[36]

In this way you create a place where learning can take place. A place where the anxiety caused by change can be addressed: the agenda is derived from the task the team is tackling; the space is not filled by the manager or team leader; groups accept that silence falls at set intervals and do not fill them with speaking; the resistances to change reveal themselves.[37] And because the social defense mechanism is acknowledged, the fixed mindset disappears and the outside can be viewed with an open mind. An organized change conviction breaks through the collective autopilot. What

35 This exercise is my adaptation of examples given in: Weick and Sutcliffe, *Managing the Unexpected*: 144-45.
36 Robert Kegan and Lisa Laskow Lahey, *How the Way We Talk Can Change the Way We Work* (San Francisco: Jossey-Bass, 2001). 102.
37 Alastair Bain, "Social Defenses against Organizational Learning," *Human Relations* 51, no. 3 (1998): 423-24.

can be said, thought and felt is different from before, in fact a conscious response.[38]

Judgmental culture	Learning culture
• Care for winners and losers; this takes energy *out* of the system	• Gives valuable information that somebody's action has meaning; puts energy *in* the system
• Indirect communication: something is said about somebody and not to somebody	• Communicates appreciation directly to the person
• General statement without much information about what the speaker appreciates	• Communicates specific information to the person about the personal experience of the speaker
• Typecasts the other	• Characterizes the experience of the speaker, does not make a caricature of the person who is appreciated
• Follows fixed formulae; nonchalant	• Sincere and authentic; more hesitant and original
• No encouragement to change	• Potential for change

In this way compassion, empathy in action, can be an important element in modern mindful teamwork. That is something other than helping each other feel good or covering team behavior with the smell of roses. Then things have gone too far and you can better avoid that.[39] In essence, compassion is about knowing how to work with each other to get the job done. With the courage to name things honestly you develop, in the green zone, a sharp but positive performance culture in your team. Compassionate performance is nowhere near as soft as you thought.

38 Ibid.
39 Michael Carroll, *Mindfulness in leiderschap* (Kampen: Ten Have, 2008). 129.

Responsibility and stewardship

Mindful management of your team begins by taking responsibility: do you dare accompany your team into the green zone of mindful teamwork? And if you do, what does your role look like?

I would like to pause at the attitude of responsibility, the intention with which you set to work. As manager, do you allow circumstances to rule or do you take the lead? Do you choose unconditionally to ensure that your own resilience is up to the mark, so that your team can also build on you or do you neglect the balance in your life? Do you dare to adopt an encouraging attitude towards emotions, both your own or in the team? Or do you prefer to keep the lid on everything? Do you choose we-communication in your team or do you let everything go its own way? Do you choose compassionate performance or a hard judgmental culture?

Naturally, there are all sorts of circumstances you could suggest in your daily work over which you have no control. A colleague has fallen ill, a department elsewhere is performing poorly, suppliers who do not keep their agreements, matters in your personal life. But you always have a choice. A simple example. If you drop a pen and ask others why the pen fell, you can get two answers. One will say that it is because of gravity, the other that you dropped the pen. If you want to prevent the pen falling again, it doesn't help to blame gravity. Then only your actions count. But often we think like this in organizations and that has become ingrained in the culture. It is precisely that choice that you have in every situation that means that you can call responsibility unconditional. No matter how difficult or awkward the situation may be, you have, as manager, the freedom to choose in all circumstances.[40] Below I summarize the choices you have between the autopilot and the green zone of mindful teamwork:

Unrelenting honesty and compassion thrive in a culture of we-communication: openness and trust, with clear language.[41] Making mistakes is permitted. Sharing information, both factual and

40 Fred Kofman, *Bewust in zaken* (Haarlem: Altamira-Becht, 2008). 69.
41 Weick and Sutcliffe, *Managing the Unexpected*: 125-26.

Teamwork on autopilot	Green zone of mindful teamwork	Manager's role
General		**Direct team attention**
Fixation on objectives	Focus on aspirations	
Me-communication	We-communication	
Fault lies with others outside the team	Take responsibility as team	
Do without overview	Know what you are doing	
Resilience		**Keeping resilience up to standard**
Stress and burn-out inevitable	Resilience and balance	
Action has priority over reflection	Regularly switching between action and reflection	
Imbalance between introversion and extroversion	Balance between introversion and extroversion	
Emotional intelligence		**See through emotions and bring them in play**
Only rational thinking important	Use emotional intelligence	
Plaster over awkward situations	Set to work with awkward situations	
Culture of dialogue		**Creating culture of dialogue**
Downloading	Open mind	
Climb the ladder: only argue and debate	Descend the ladder: investigate and dialogue	
Vertical decision-making	Horizontal dialogue	

Feedback as criticism	Feedback as on-going care for what can be improved	
Debate culture (win or lose)	Dialogue culture (win-win)	
Compassionate performance		**Embody compassion and learning**
Focused only on results	Focused on results and collaboration	
Achieving objectives is the work	Delivering results is the fruit of teamwork	
Reject sympathy (empathic stress)	Sympathize and change (compassion)	
Judgmental culture	Culture of learning and coaching	

emotional, is crucial in this, as is sharing fairly and accepting the responsibility for a mistake or near failure. A harsh judgmental culture does not help here. Also because it prevents skillfully dealing with necessary adjustments under pressure or change of tempo in work, and a judgmental culture puts the brakes on learning processes.

You could perhaps best see your role as manager as that of a steward. Good stewardship with appreciation for the performances achieved, stated from your own experience, specifically directed at a person. And stewardship in naming awkward matters and not plastering them over. In your role as manager of a team, you can introduce stewardship in the green zone of mindfulness and thus promote compassionate performance.

References

Adams, Juliet. "The Business Case for Mindfulness in the Work-place: A Guide to Promoting Mindfulness to Corporate Clients." 1-46: Mindfulnet.org, 2012.

Argyris, Chris. *Overcoming Organizational Defenses*. Upper Saddle River New jersey: Prentice Hall, 1990.

Bain, Alastair. "Social Defenses Against Organizational Learning." *Human Relations* 51, no. 3 (1998): 413-29.

Boyatzis, Richard, and Annie McKee. *Resonant Leadership*. Cambridge: Harvard Business Press, 2005.

Brink, Erik van den, and Frits Koster. *Compassievol leven. Van mindfulness naar heartfulness*. Amsterdam: Boom, 2012.

Carroll, Michael. *Mindfulness in leiderschap*. Kampen: Ten Have, 2008.

Chapman, Susan. *The Five Keys to Mindful Communication*. Boston: Shambhala, 2012.

Goleman, Daniel. *Working with Emotional Intelligence*. New York: Bantam Books, 1998.

Goleman, Daniel, Richard Boyatzis, and Annie McKee. *Primal Leadership. Realizing the Power of Emotional Intelligence*. Boston: Harvard Business School Press, 2002.

Katzenbach, Jon R., and Douglas K. Smith. *Het geheim van teams. Een organisatie van wereldklasse creëren*. Schiedam: Scriptum, 1997.

Kegan, Robert, and Lisa Laskow Lahey. *How the Way We Talk Can Change the Way We Work*. San Francisco: Jossey-Bass, 2001.

Kets de Vries, Manfred. *Het egel effect*. Den Haag: Academic Service, 2012.

Kleiner, Art, and Rutger von Post. "A Corporate Climate of Mutual Help." *Strategy + Business*, no. 62 (Spring 2011 2011): 11-14.

Kofman, Fred. *Bewust in zaken*. Haarlem: Altamira-Becht, 2008.

Kramer, Gregory. *Insight Dialogue*. Boston: Shambhala, 2007.

Maex, Edel. *Open mind. Anders kijken naar de werkelijkheid*. Gent: Witsand Uitgevers, 2009.

Melville, Geoffrey W., Dennis Chang, Ben Colagiuri, Paul W. Marshall, and Birinder S. Cheema. "Fifteen Minutes of Chair-Based Yoga Postures or Guided Meditation Performed in the

Office Can Elicit a Relaxations Response." *Evidence-Based Complementary and Alternative Medicine* 2012 (2012): 1-9.

Pink, Daniel H. *Drive*. Amsterdam: Business Contact, 2010.

Price, Andrew. *Slow Tech. Manifesto for an Overwound World*. London: Atlantic Books, 2009.

Ridings, Amanda. *Pause for Breath*. London: Live it Publishing, 2011.

Ruedy, Nicole E., and Maurice E. Schweitzer. "In the Moment: The Effect of Mindfulness on Ethical Decision Making." *Journal of Business Ethics* 95 (2010): 75-87.

Scharmer, C. Otto. *Theorie U. Leiding vanuit de toekomst die zich aandient*. Zeist: Christofoor, 2010.

Schein, Edgar H. *Helping*. San Francisco: Berrett-Koehler, 2009.

Senge, Peter. *De noodzakelijke revolutie*. Den Haag: Academic Service, 2009.

———. *De vijfde discipline*. Schiedam: Scriptum, 1992.

Tan, Chade-Meng. *Search Inside Yourself*. New York: HarperCollins, 2012.

Ulrich, Dave, and Wendy Ulrich. *Het waarom van werk. Naar een organisatie van overvloed*. Amsterdam: Business Contact, 2011.

Weick, Karl E., and Kathleen M. Sutcliffe. *Managing the Unexpected*. San Francisco: John Wiley & Sons, 2010.

5

Charting a course with full attention

*"From a mindful perspective one's response to a particular
situation is not an attempt to make the best choice from
amongst available options but to create options."*[1]

Ellen Langer – *The Power of Mindful Learning*

In the previous chapters, I have laid the foundation for the use of
our capacity for mindfulness both individually and in teams. Now
we are going to look at how you can use mindfulness within the
organization in the process of value creation for customers and
stakeholders.

If mindfulness is anchored in the culture of the company, the
organization is capable of switching attention in an effective way:
now attention for the operational quality, meaning more focused
on the way in which the current products and services should be
delivered, and then focusing the attention on the challenges for
the organization or the system to which it belongs and which demand innovation.

I start this chapter with the question of how you can get a picture of how mindful an organization is. Then I will deal extensive-
ly with how an organization can learn to juggle four fields of attention, which are based on the four ways of listening and conversing
that I described in the previous chapters. In the last part of this
chapter, we return to the question of how to anchor mindfulness
in an organization. That it is about culture change and is always

1 Ellen Langer, *The Power of Mindful Learning* (Cambridge: Perseus Books,
1997), 113-14.

part of a larger process aimed at creating value for the customer.[2] And if one thing is clear from professional literature about organizational culture and change, it is that you cannot change the culture of an organization by itself and isolated from environment, aim, and strategy of the organization. The role of mindful leadership will prove crucial in that.[3]

Mindfulness in the organization

Before we take a look at how you can organize directing attention in an organization, it is worthwhile getting an initial picture of how mindful the organization you work in really is. That is not the same as a thorough culture analysis of the organization; more is needed for that. And, as Schein correctly stated, questionnaires and checklists are insufficient because they do not reveal the deep-rooted common assumptions in a culture.[4] Those deep-rooted common assumptions also contain the power of the immunity to change, which I discussed in the first chapter. Even though you will not get a complete picture of the autopilot and the mechanism of immunity in the culture of your organization, you will get a first picture.

You can start by going back to the overview table about the green zone of mindfulness, which I presented at the end of the previous chapter, and scoring your organization on this. Where is your organization in each of the dimensions? More toward the autopilot or more toward mindful team work? Is attention paid to resilience, emotional intelligence, we-communication, and compassionate performance? Or is your organization still completely on the side of the judgmental culture? The core question is perhaps: do you, as an organization know what you're doing, both about what you are delivering in products or services and what is

2 Jaap Boonstra, *Leiders in cultuurverandering*, Stichting Management Studies (Assen: Van Gorcum, 2011), 313.

3 Jelle Dijkstra and Paul-Peter Feld, *Gedeeld leiderschap: veerkacht door nieuwe vormen van samenwerken, organiseren, leren en leiderschap* (2012).

4 Edgar H. Schein, *De bedrijfscultuur als ziel van de onderneming* (Schiedam: Scriptum, 2008), 60.

necessary in innovation, and is there sufficient presence of mind in the organization to break free of the autopilot and to recognize the immunity mechanisms?

Once you have done that, you can add to your picture using the questionnaire below, which is directed at how closely you monitor the work processes. This list comes from the influential study by Weick and Sutcliffe into organizations that demand a high reliability of operational processes.[5] In nine so-called audits, they try to get a picture of the condition of an organization where reliability is necessary and where mindfulness should be on the agenda. That focus on high reliability also implies the limitation of it, for reliability and combating mistakes is not the first priority in all organizations. But you can, with a few adjustments, also use the questionnaire for other organizations. You can, for example, think of "deviating events" as "quality that does not satisfy the standard" and you can consider "concerns about misinterpreting events" as "trying to fathom what are the reasons or causes of successes and failures" or as "being able to read and listen between the lines." That is why I have chosen to use the questionnaire in its original form.

A picture of the mindfulness of your organization
How well do the following statements describe your organization?
For each item, fill in 1, 2, or 3
1 = absolutely not; 2 = partially; 3 = to a large degree

	1	2	3
1. Throughout the organization there is a feeling of being receptive to the unexpected.	....	....	....
2. Everybody feels responsible for reliability.	....	....	....
3. Management gives as much attention to managing the unexpected as to achieving formal organization objectives.	....	....	....
4. At all levels in our organization, people are constantly concerned about deviating events.	....	....	....

---

5   Karl E. Weick and Kathleen M. Sutcliffe, *Managing the Unexpected* (San Francisco: John Wiley & Sons, 2010), 87.

5. At all levels in our organization, people are constantly ....
   concerned about misidentifying events.
6. At all levels in our organization, people are   ....
   constantly concerned about misunderstanding events.
7. We spend time on identifying how our activities could ....
   potentially damage all our stakeholders.
8. There is widespread agreement among the people   ....
   in our organization that we do not want to make
   any mistakes.
9. There is widespread agreement among the people   ....
   in our organization about how things can go wrong.

Determine the score by adding up the figures. If you score higher
than 17, the culture of mindfulness is good in your organization.
A score between 11 and 17 means that you are on the way to
building such a culture. If the score is lower than 11, there's a lot of
work to be done.

This table is based on a study into nuclear energy plants and the
management of the electricity network. It showed that the more
people in the organization are actively involved in identifying, precisely describing, and combating misinterpretations, the higher the
reliability of the organization.[6] The same was shown in the examples
of the surgical teams in hospitals that function better when they report mistakes. Mindfulness thus leads to better and more reliable
performances and prevents organizations becoming bogged down
in daily routines. They are at least aware of the autopilot.

That was not the case with one of my clients, where I investigated
why the organization had seemed to come to a standstill. Renewal
of the organization seemed an almost impossible task. Firm decisions were not easily taken, all layers of the organization had to be
fully involved first. And when, after considerable upheaval, the decision was finally made, there was little sign of any implementation. My study showed that management and employees had their
very unique way of dealing with each other, which I classified as

6 Ibid.

"kind and tepid." On the one hand, people were very friendly to each other, there was no sharp feedback on each other's work and mistakes were generally blamed on circumstances. Rather kind, in fact. But also tepid, for people's involvement in the results of the work and with each other and with the way everybody functioned was not particularly great. And so it had become an organization that couldn't move forwards or backwards.

What was lacking was that they did not dare see the reality in its naked truth. Only when I confronted them with this – with here and there a smile of recognition on their face – did it get through to them: yes, this was the way they were... The example shows how an organization can get bogged down in everyday activities – before you know it, you are working in a sick organization, where the attention is completely drained away towards internal problems. People have lost sight of what they are doing. And it is not that easy to escape from that culture.

Another example shows that an organization can also become bogged down because new events are simplified into well-known interpretations or mental models. I remember as if it were yesterday that, immediately after the attacks in New York on 11 September 2001, the membership drive by the Dutch Consumers' Association, where I was working as manager at the time, fell apart. The familiar mailings no longer worked, the new applications dried up almost completely. Our first interpretation was that people just didn't feel the need at that time to take out a membership with the association nor did they feel the need for information about quality and prices of products and services. But the effectiveness of mailings did not return to their former level, even after the main tension around 9/11 had subsided.

Little by little, there was room for new interpretations: there was apparently something else happening, the emergence of Internet had superseded the old way of reaching potential customers, and what's more, people no longer wanted a paper membership but a digital membership. I still remember how we struggled to let go of the well-known interpretations and search for new explanations. The old way of thinking was still in our heads.

By introducing a climate of attention, of a green zone of mindfulness, you have already taken a step toward avoiding finding yourself in such a situation. There is a far greater attention and re-silience under pressure of circumstances in the day-to-day work. And you can now, as a mindful a leader, use that basis to shape with full attention the relationship your organization has with customers and stakeholders.

Focusing the attention of organizations

It is very important for organizations to be clear about how they are creating value for their customers. And the importance of this is again underlined by the fact that organizations – whether they deliver products or services – increasingly find themselves reaching their limits, because they need others for their production process, or have to deal with their social environment and stakeholders, who watch critically over their shoulders. At the same time, it is necessary that attention continue to be paid to what is happening in the existing organization, their operational excellence. Organizations and networks must learn to switch between various forms of attention, between what must happen here and now, and react with an open mind to what the future asks of them.

When learning that switching, organizations can, in addition to the pitfalls mentioned in the previous chapter, easily fall into other pitfalls when the attention is directed to what is happening outside the organization. Traps when developing strategies. A short summary:

1. Dynamic conservatism: considerable effort, but the patterns in the organization remain the same *(keep falling into habit patterns)*
2. Daydreams: the assumptions behind the strategy are incorrect *(debate about differences but no fundamental solution)*
3. Drawing-board models: the story is correct but it finds no connection in the organization, it is handled in a totally non-committal way *(connection with the other, but no real consequences drawn)*
4. Lost strategies: valuable directions that do not reach the mainstream and therefore remain unused *(good story but no depth).*[7]

7 Paul Kloosterboer, "Navigeren bij strategievorming, lessen uit de literatuur," *M&O*, no. 5 (2008).

EMPHASIS ON THE PARTS

OPEN MINDSET: DESIGN NEW WORK METHODS

IV. INNOVATION AND EXPERIMENTATION
Ecosystem
Logic: penetrating system innovation

Generative dialogue: discovering the new between the lines
- Searching for larger questions of the future

Attention: from what is going to come, open, without world view

Downloading or habit listening: routine
- Repeating existing thought patterns

Attention: from yourself as the midpoint; fixed world view

III. RECOGNIZING PATTERNS IN BROADER WHOLE
Matrix organization, stakeholder relationships
Logic: innovation advantages (product innovation)

Empathic conversing: you shift yourself into the other's position
- Advocacy and inquiry in balance
- Reflection

Attention: from the position of the other; you leave your own world view

Attention: from the edge of your own world view without affecting it

Debate: observe differences
- Winning or losing; arguing

II. USING DIFFERENCES: QUALITY IMPROVEMENT
Departments, industry sectors, satisfying market
Logic: scope advantages (customer)

I. MONITORING THE EXECUTION
Hierarchy, bureaucracy, following rules
Logic: upscaling (production)

FIXED MINDSET: REPEATING PATTERNS FROM THE PAST

EMPHASIS ON THE WHOLE

Organizing with full attention means that you learn to avoid these pitfalls. Otto Scharmer has developed a model distinguishing four "fields of attention" in organizations (and it also applies to networks and alliances). He also calls them fields of conversation or social interaction, because the difference between one way of talking to each other or working on challenges (such as developing new strategies or leveraging more intensive teamwork or innovation) and another has to do with whether attention is focused on the now or on the future and more on the whole or on individual parts.[8]

In the model, two axes are distinguished: one axis is the perspective from which you look at the situation. Are you looking more from the individual parts or are you looking more from the whole. The other axis is whether you are looking from a more fixed context, do you remain – largely – within the existing framework or do you look from a more open view of the situation. In this way, four forms of attention emerge. If a simple problem must be solved, it can be sufficient to repeat the current situation or critically compare available information . But anybody wanting to organize profound change will discover that it is necessary to let go of the existing mindset completely. I shall briefly characterize the four forms below:

I. MONITORING THE EXECUTION
In the first field, *downloading* or habitual action is the way of conversing and social interaction. The attention is completely directed from your own midpoint and assumes your own world view. You work from the existing context and that is a fixed fact. The organization follows the execution of its own production processes. By occasionally pausing and being observant, a first form of alertness is achieved in an otherwise routine-like culture.

8   C. Otto Scharmer, *Theorie U. Leiding vanuit de toekomst die zich aandient* (Zeist: Christofoor, 2010), 323. I use the model in the form developed by Peter Senge, *De noodzakelijke revolutie* (Den Haag: Academic Service, 2009), 239.

II. USING DIFFERENCES: QUALITY IMPROVEMENT
In the second field of *debate*, the attention shifts to the edge or the peripheral region of your own world, you look where differences from the existing norms are and act with others, without subjecting your own world view to the discussion. You are fully aware of where the differences in relation to fellow departments, other companies or competitors are and have the courage to learn from these differences. In this field, an organization has a way of keeping a sharp eye on developments starting from its own world view, of fully appreciating the difference between itself and others and learning from it. An organization that operates sharply and attentively in this by having the ability to face reality and not to hide behind an ideal picture or some magnificent vision.[9] It is all about operational excellence.

III. RECOGNISING PATTERNS IN BROADER WHOLE
In the following field, that of *empathic conversing*, the attention of the organization is directed from the position of the other in the work field, the network, or the system. It leaves its own world view and empathizes with that of somebody else or of another organization. The strength of this type of attention is that this organization – but it also equally applies for a network or group of stakeholders – is capable of fathoming the patterns in the external environment and its own role therein.

IV. INNOVATION AND EXPERIMENTATION
In the fourth field of *generative dialogue*, the organization is prepared to address the challenges and give them shape without working from their own interests, but instead from what is required from the common situation of the organization or the group of organizations.[10] In this field there is systematic attention for innovation and experimentation, whereby, thanks to design thinking, it is capable of anticipating largely uncertain futures.

9 Daniel Goleman, Richard Boyatzis, and Annie McKee, *Primal Leadership. Realizing the Power of Emotional Intelligence* (Boston: Harvard Business School Press, 2002), 172.
10 Scharmer, *Theorie U. Leiding vanuit de toekomst die zich aandient*, 281-88.

Every organization and the individuals in it have (although they do not always realize it), to a lesser or greater degree, access to each of the four sources or fields of attention. And for each field of attention there are a number of working ways or methods with which the organizations can handle issues in that field. Below I have indicated, for each of the four fields, which organizational practices are suitable.

The first field: eye for routine-breaking moments

In the first field, mindfulness supports building up the ability to focus attention on monitoring the execution by having an eye for moments that have broken that routine. To stop the autopilot or simply continue working because everything has to be completed, and to look to see whether the patterns that are expected are actually in play.

A good way of making a start with that in an organization is to regularly map the *wake-up calls*. An example of a wake-up call can be that you, as management consultant, are working on a bid with a client. It is about a big assignment for supporting a strategy process of a housing corporation. Initially the client is enthusiastic. But then the following appointment is cancelled. You do not react because you are overloaded with other things, you just sit and wait. After a few weeks, you phone again. The client tells you that it can take some time, without further explanation. Only when a colleague mentions during a work consultation that this corporation is in financial problems (he read it in the newspaper) do you start to see the light. At the first meeting, the director of the corporation had mentioned that this was mainly for the long term, and that they had to become financially healthy again. You had ignored that signal, because your focus was on the strategy process. If only we had picked up on these signals, you think. In the future, it is perhaps useful to discuss new assignments with your colleagues...

Mapping wake-up calls
Take half an hour at a team meeting to pause at clearly visible, but also slowly developing changes in the operational processes and

the environment of the organization. For this, you can best start by a few minutes of silence in which you shift the attention to remembering this type of moment. Next, get the team to write down all wake-up calls on post-its and one by one to state them and explain them. Then discuss what can be learned from these wake-up calls.

Examples of wake-up calls:
- An assignment for a client doesn't go ahead
- A change in sickness absence patterns
- Losing material or tools
- A new competitor in the market
- A malfunction of the telephone or Internet in the organization
- New types of complaints from customers
- Delivery of goods arriving too late
- Small quarrels between employees in the team
- Etcetera...

Another method is the check-in. We saw this previously with teamwork in the operating theater. In some organizations, there is a formal moment of handover, such as in hospitals, at security locations, or with the police. Such moments help to inform each other about what is happening. It can be highly effective to set up such moments for organizations that do not have such formal handovers.

This way of working, in which you build in a conscious silence and attention, can also improve the quality of formal handover moments. Conscious attention for what the organization is doing sharpens the organization's mental switching ability between doing and being. You set the tone for the way of operating in the organization. Furthermore, you consciously pause to recognize the mental condition in which the team is operating and that filters through in the emotional intelligence of the team.

Check-in
The check-in is part of the daily routine of a department or team. At the start of the day or – if that proves difficult – during the first coffee break, take 15 minutes to pause to consider how the group is.

This method is aimed at revealing where the attention of the group is and to direct it to the here and now.

The check-in starts with a short, open question focused on the experience of the moment. That can, for example, be the answer to questions such as:

- What am I doing?
- What is becoming clearer to me?
- How am I feeling now?
- Which issues are occupying me at the moment?

Ask the people to answer from their own experience, not with a sentence or expression suggesting an idea or an opinion. It is, after all, about acknowledging what is happening, not what they think of it.[11]

You can allow the answering to take place in the *order of the circle*, and, if you like, with a *talking piece* or using the *popcorn* method, in which people speak when they are ready. If a silence falls, that is okay. Allow the sharing to take place quietly, without any time pressure. You will be surprised how quickly it happens. People do not have to react to each other, their own story is enough.

The answers can give the group and the manager insight into what is occupying them at that moment and whether perhaps there are matters that have to be addressed or solved for collaboration to be fruitful. But also successes, joys and sorrows can be shared. As manager or facilitator of the group, you can, at the end, hold the matters that have struck you up to the group, so that the picture of what is happening is strengthened. Always make room here for additions.

If such ways of working are used regularly, even daily, then alertness emerges in the organization which increases the resilience against continuing to work thoughtlessly in a routine. Some organizations make use not only of a check-in but also a conscious check-out. Both help with working with greater awareness.

Incidentally, it is not necessary for everybody to be together at the office at the same time for a check-in or check-out. They can

11 For a good summary of the difference between thoughts and feelings, see: Marshall B. Rosenberg, *Geweldloze communicatie* (Rotterdam: Lemniscaat, 2007), 57-60.

also be done with people working at different places, using cloud working. I regularly hold an international Skype call with colleagues for such a check-in. That works very well and surprisingly enough, a call without video often works better because the visual distraction is less and the attention can be more easily directed at the content and "tone of voice" of the others. But you can also check-in via the chat feature on Skype or Facebook, and even a check-in conversation via e-mail, where there is a time difference in answering, can work very well. Plenty of options.

The second field: using differences

In the second field, mindfulness ensures that the attention is directed at how the organization functions in comparison to the previously set internal norms or to other organizations. In the first case we generally talk about evaluation of operational processes, and in the second case of benchmarking of our own organization in comparison with the best performing organization in the same industry. In both cases, however, the existing situation is the starting point in distinguishing the differences. The mindset is fixed and from that mindset you set about improving processes.

For that you need to develop a view that is as sharp and broad as possible, but your field of vision remains limited to your own world view. Notice that I intentionally used the expression *distinguishing view* and not the word *concentration*. Concentration suggests that you shut things out. This doesn't mean it is bad, but you use it in a different situation, namely when you are occupied with a task. But if people are too concentrated, there is too little attention for the question of whether the organization works well from different perspectives.[12] A mindful organization ensures that the edges of its own field of vision are observed. There the differences are clearest.

For the development of a discerning view, an organization must be capable of dealing honestly and open-heartedly with itself, the unrelenting honesty that belongs with compassionate perfor-

12 Weick and Sutcliffe, *Managing the Unexpected*, 87-88.

mance. In such a culture, every employee and manager can talk about the mistakes or errors that he or she has made without being immediately punished for it. On the contrary, reporting errors deserves to be rewarded. There is a story about the famous German rocket scientist, Werner von Braun, who stood at the cradle of the German rockets in the Second World War and of the American space program. He sent a bottle of champagne to an employee who had reported that he might, during a test prior to a launch of a rocket which subsequently exploded, have caused a short circuit. After further analysis, his report was shown to be true and because he had reported it, enormous costs were saved for expensive new designs. Research into teams of nurses in hospitals suggested that teams that performed better reported more mistakes than those that performed more poorly. The climate of openness was stronger and that allowed mistakes to be reported and rectified more quickly. In addition, people appeared to learn quicker from openly discussing mistakes.[13]

An organization that works mindfully supports the open view with systematic evaluation and checking of operational processes. I discuss here two ways of working; both are practical and easily executed: the operational evaluation, and the debriefing. Both are part of the tool box of this type of organization, in which the first concentrates on uncovering mistakes, the second gets an overview of everything that happens, both in the process and in the people who participate in it.

Operational evaluation[14]

You can apply this type of evaluation to gain insight into the way processes in your organization actually work. It can be about a failed bid, an appointment that was not kept, a project that contained both successes and several important errors, various interpretations of a question, changed attitude of a collaborating partner, and so on. The in-

---

13 Ibid., 50-51.
14 This exercise is my own adaptation of the Evaluating without Blame exercise in: Bert van Dalen, Bert Slagmolen, and Robert Taen, *Mindful organiseren* (Apollo 13 Consult, 2009), 106.

tention is most certainly not to apportion guilt, but to discover what
can be learned from an unexpected event.

You can use the structure of this exercise during a meeting or at a
separate session. The duration depends on the size of the evaluated
event and varies from half an hour to an hour.

Begin by reconstructing the time line (or time lines, from the perspective of various participants) of the event. Ensure that people
can work with an open mind and with attention. It helps to start the
session with several minutes to "get in touch" through a meditative
exercise and then to work in silence individually on the reconstruc-
tion of the time line.

Each time line states:

- The concrete steps in the event. Ensure that these can be ob-
  served.
- The actions of each participating person
- Ask why each person did what he did (observable)
- And which interpretations and thoughts he had (both thoughts
  and feelings, thus experiences)
- How one action anticipated the other (cause and result)

Then look back and investigate where interpretations and suppositions differed in the persons participating in the event.

State what can be learned from this.

And together think what can be done differently the next time.

An example can clarify how such an operational evaluation works.
After a major publicity campaign, the non-governmental organization I worked with was extremely satisfied with the media cover-
age. The director was interviewed on two television channels, various newspapers had written about it. In short, there was quite a bit
of media attention. And yet there was something not quite right,
because the strategists who contacted the members of the Dutch
parliament noticed that the message was not getting through. Was
something missing?

The team decided to carry out an evaluation and set out the
course of the whole campaign in a timeline. When everything was
finally on the flip chart and a dialogue had taken place, it emerged
that there were two different frameworks for interpreting the suc-

cess of the campaign. For the communication people, it was visibility in the media, for the lobbyists, the adoption of the organization's opinions by members of parliament. For the communication people, it was logical that communications should first take place in the media and that members of parliament were then approached. The lobbyists had not realized that the members of parliament preferred to be informed of the lobby standpoints before the media. Both components were in the campaign, but a planning mistake and time pressure meant that the letter with the brochure for members of parliament was not ready at the start of the media campaign. The result was that the members of parliament learned of the demands from the media and reacted rather reticently. That was because they had not been informed in advance about the campaign and the demands of the organization. When asked for their reasons, the members of parliament reacted rather reticently that they preferred not to be taken by surprise. The results of the campaign suffered under a difference in interpretation about success and an error of timing.

A form of developing a broader perspective, which can also be usefully applied, is the debriefing of events or processes. In a debriefing, it is all about gaining insight into everything that happens around the process in which the event takes place. It is thus a consciously deployed way of not only looking at the content of a series of actions from the perspective of success or failure, but also at how the process unfolds and everything that has an influence on it. In this, the personal experiences, of the participants in the process are explicitly included.

Debriefing: seeing different perspectives and learning experiences

A debriefing is used to evaluate how a process unfolds. You can actually consider it part of Kolb's learning cycle: first gain experience, then observe what happened, then debrief, and subsequently draw conclusions about how to do it the next time.

Begin a debriefing with the request to the participants to spend five or ten minutes noting down in silence all the experiences they observed as the process of the event unfolded. When we talk here about a process, this can be a piece of work, for example the execution of a lobby action, the joint execution of a campaign, assistance to a client, a training session, etcetera. It is also useful to point out to the participants at the debriefing that experiences can relate to both visible characteristics and parts of the way the process unfolded and to the inner experience of the participants in it. With an attitude of mindfulness, we include thoughts, feelings, physical sensations and actions, or the urge to take action, in our experience.

Next you share in the group the experiences of how the project unfolded. It is important that no perspective whatsoever is excluded. Every learning experience is valid and neither better nor worse than any other.
Then the participants write down their individual conclusions and their own learning experiences from what has been brought to the fore.
The manager/facilitator then collects the conclusions, possible learning experiences, and/or points of improvement.

Operational evaluation and debriefing are effective ways to gain insight into the processes in the organization. A participant in one of the teams with which I worked:

> *"What strikes me in this debriefing is that I learn how you can look at our assistance to the client from various perspectives. There is not just one certainty or one way of doing things well. And at the same time you see that our experiences all circle around a core that leads to the result. The result is co-creation. And I learn from the approach of colleagues."*

In addition to the two ways of evaluation described above, with which you gain insight into routine behavior and its effects (the autopilot), it is, in this second field of attention, using differences, also usual to look at deeper rooted resistance to change when it has become clear what must be changed. In this way, the immunity to change is also addressed. Chris Argyris recently summarized the lessons he has learned in a lifetime of research into this in his book

Organizational Traps. This book contains a number of examples of expressions that hide a deep-rooted resistance. You encounter them every day in organizations:[15]

> *"They simply don't understand it."*
> *"You can never be honest with them – they immediately become defensive."*
> *"They lead the meeting as if everybody has a say in the decision, but in reality they've already drawn their conclusions."*
> *"Of course I can't say it straight to his face."*
> *"Bob never listens – if you want to get anything done, you have to go round him"*
> *"Nothing ever changes here."*

Pitfalls such as these can have unfortunate and even damaging consequences. Teachers then help pupils pass their exams because that increases the school's income. The accident with the space shuttle Columbia happened despite the fact that an earlier report about the Challenger shuttle had stated exactly what could go wrong and those recommendations were also implemented.

What is interesting is that even when people feel trapped in a pitfall, they are no weak-willed victims: their own behavior contributes to being in it. We create pitfalls for ourselves if we make issues uncomfortable or threatening for everybody. They make it easy to place the blame outside ourselves and thus prevent us from learning. And that is why recognizing patterns and pitfalls is so important for directing attention. With mindfulness you are much better able to see what is happening and you gain insight more quickly into the difference between behavior that you display and the story that you tell yourselves and others about it. And that is a first condition for change. Argyris and Schön have thought up a method that helps people in organizations to uncover the silent patterns in conversations and behavior in the organization and to start a discussion about them. It is known as the left column method.

---

15 Chris Argyris, *Organizational Traps* (Oxford: Oxford University Press, 2010), 2.

The left column method[16]
The exercise uses the description of an event or a situation to help you gain insight into the underlying patterns, the silent assumptions, in the mutual behavior of an organization. In this form, it takes about half an hour.

Step 1
Describe in a couple of sentences a situation that is crucial for you and which you would like to solve in a more productive way.

Step 2
Imagine you can set to work freely with those involved in a way that is, according to you, productive. What would you do or say to those individuals in a way that would mean progress? Write a few paragraphs about it.

Step 3
Imagine that you are holding such a discussion or know that one will soon take place.
Divide your paper into two halves. In the right column you write down what you said (or are going to say in a future conversation). Write it down in the way you would for a play or a dialogue. Literally. And also write down what the other said or what you think the other will answer. Here again, be literal – use the actual words. In this way, you build up a report of the conversation in the right column.
Incidentally, do not worry whether you have written everything down precisely enough. What is important is that it is, in your opinion, as close as possible to the reality.

Step 4
In the left column you write down all feelings, physical experiences, sensations, and thoughts that you had internally during the conver-

16 This short description is derived from: ibid., 27-28 He also gives several examples of cases. You can find a very lively description of the method and approach in: Peter Senge et al., *De vijfde discipline. Praktijkboek* (Den Haag: Academic Service, 2006), 212-18.

sation, but which you never expressed. You do not have to explain why you did not express them.

After a page or, at most, two, you are virtually finished.

Leave the exercise aside for a few days and then look at it again. You can then ask the following questions:
- Why is it that I think like this and feel like this?
- What was my intention? What did I try to achieve?
- Did I achieve the desired result?
- Could my comments have aggravated the problems?
- What withheld me from a different approach?
- How can I use my left column as a way of improving our communications?

If you are to progress further, you must write down the conversation again, but then in a way that you think is more effective. You can share it with colleagues.

If you apply this way of working in a group, a good facilitator can help lead the conversation about the situation and the group's left columns.

You can achieve two things with the left column method: a) understanding and explaining whether the intentions of your actions match the actions themselves; and b) empirical testing can show whether the prediction you made about the results of the conversation actually came about. Both give you insight into the underlying mental model that you used to equip your actions with arguments and to plan.[17]

The examples given above are particularly aimed at distinguishing the differences with regard to the norms stipulated internally. Benchmarking in its many forms is aimed exactly at discovering the differences between the way an organization functions and the

17 The left column method described above is for an individual in an organisation. William Noonan has designed a template for how you can use it in a group. It is called the Action-Impact template. See: William R. Noonan, *Discussing the Undiscussable. A Guide to Overcoming Defensive Routines in the Workplace* (San Francisco: Jossey-Bass, 2007). From 228.

"best practices" of similar organizations, and so improve its own functioning. There are many well-known methods of measuring and comparing, of which the SWOT analysis is the best known. The risk of benchmarking is, however, that you continue looking within the existing mindset and do not see that fundamental changes have occurred in the environment of the industry in which you are comparing yourself.

The third field: recognizing patterns in a broader whole

In the third field of attention, we make the transition from a more closed mindset, in which the attention of the organization remains with the existing world view, into a more open mindset, which observes the surroundings and ultimately also the still unknown future. In this field, we build from mindfulness the capacity to recognize patterns and to take a view of the broader system in which an organization operates.

A good way of gaining insight into patterns is by giving attention to the system of which the organization is a part or the system within the organization, certainly if that is somewhat larger. Systems thinking is a way of learning to see the whole. You start looking at the mutual relationships between parts instead of at parts in isolation. This teaches you to see patterns of change. It is comparable with the change from a normal MRI scan, which photographs dozens of "layers" in the brain and thus builds up a static image of it, to that of an fMRI scan, a functional MRI scan, that makes a moving image of the brain. Systems thinking arose at the end of the last century in a wide area of science and was introduced into the world of organizational science by Peter Senge in his book *The Fifth Discipline*. It was developed earlier in the previous century from cybernetic concepts about feedback and servo-mechanic engineering. It demands a special sensitivity for the subtle way in which things are connected to each other and from which living systems derive their unique character. He sees it as a way of better dealing with deep-rooted patterns of behavior, of complexity. Using systems thinking we can combat the undermining of our self-confidence and our feeling of responsibility engendered by complexity. It starts by learning to see circles of causality.[18]

Seeing systems

By seeing systems, you look at the underlying relationships in a whole of parts and not at those parts individually. It is applicable to situations within an organization, but particularly to relationships of an organization or several organizations within their environment. Thinking in terms of chains and alliances seems similar, but systems thinking looks even more at the deeper underlying structures.

The core of systems thinking can be summarized in a different mental attitude:

• Seeing mutual relationships instead of a linear linking of cause and effect.
• Seeing processes instead of random moments.

The crux of systems thinking is that you learn to think in *circles of causality*. By analyzing systems, you learn to understand leverage, and that can be an important point of action for steering towards a new situation.

I shall briefly illustrate systems thinking with an example from the work of Senge that I mentioned earlier but will now clarify further. More has been written elsewhere about understanding systems, including work by one of its founders, Donatella Meadows.[19]

The example refers back to the collaboration between Coca-Cola and WWF, which I described at the beginning of this book. Coca-Cola learned to see that the necessity of having a good and reliable water supply was helped with a long-term solution. In those situations you need a language in which you can name pat-

---

18 Peter Senge, *De vijfde discipline* (Schiedam: Scriptum, 1992), 73-74.
19 Donella H. Meadows, *Thinking in Systems. A Primer* (London: Earthscan, 2008). Also see: Bill Bryan, Michael Goodman, and Jaap Schaveling, *Systeemdenken. Ontdekken van onze organisatiepatronen* (Den Haag: Academic Service, 2006).

terns, of which systems thinking is one. In this way, you learn to distinguish between short-term and long-term solutions. Coca-Cola had the choice to relocate bottling plants to places with less restrictive regulation in the area of water. But such a solution is not tenable in the long term, because in many places in the world, the supply of water is a major issue. Then you have to decide not to go for the quick fix, but instead choose a more fundamental solution.[20] The difference between these two approaches is illustrated in the model below. Although the more fundamental solution seems to cause a delay, it offers many more advantages in the long term.

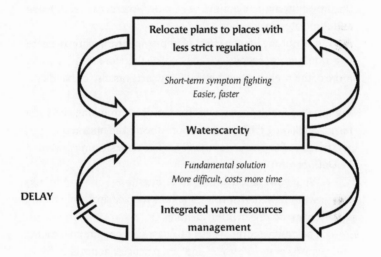

The advantage of looking at things in this way is that you can make strategic choices based on your understanding of the underlying patterns, the system.

In addition to systems thinking, there is another approach which, unlike other methods, places the emphasis on the valuable elements in an organization and the surrounding world. It looks at chances and opportunities and not so much at problems. The ap-

20 Senge, *De noodzakelijke revolutie*, 40-42.

proach is called *appreciative inquiry* and was designed in the 1980s by David Cooperrider. An important characteristic is that action, communication, and knowledge development are brought into interaction with each other, and together this produces significance.

Appreciative inquiry[21]

Appreciative inquiry is both a theory and a method. Inquiry and change going hand in hand is one of the starting points. For this, an explicit appeal is made to the intelligence and imagination in the organization. A consciously chosen positive perspective (based on the proven strength of positive psychology) sharpens that thinking and stimulates imagination.

A positive attitude has the effect of improving the quality of the interaction because people feel safer and are therefore ready to reveal more of themselves. Then "difficult" subjects can also be handled.

Appreciative inquiry steps away from problem thinking and is directed at realizing the future, it is more directed at innovation.

The process of appreciative inquiry has five stages:

1. **Define:** form a team and determine:
   - What you want to study; what questions you want to ask; who you want to involve, and how you will do it.
2. **Discover:** do research and identify:
   - The positive core; the essential factors when the core theme is at its best; core values and best practices; hopes and wishes for the future; ideas for implementation.
3. **Dream:** create a compelling vision about who we would be if we were to grow and build from the positive core and make full use of it in achieving our aims.
4. **Design:** give shape to this by: making far-reaching proposals with major impact on the performance.
5. **Deliver:** achieve the dream by honoring initiatives, valuing success, by improvising, and by learning.

21 Based on: Robert Masselink et al., *Waarderend organiseren* (Amsterdam: Gelling Publicaties, 2008).

Appreciative inquiry can be used in small-scale and large-scale contexts.

In various places, reports have been made about cases that have been addressed using the AI method. I shall deal with one here; others can be found in the literature.[22]

The division of Hunter Douglas that specializes in modern, innovative window coverings (curtains, blinds, sunshades, etc.) noticed at the start of the 1990s that employees were dissatisfied, turnover increased and the employees were so overworked that there was little room for their own initiative and contribution to innovation. The management deployed the process "Focus 2000," directed at developing vision, regeneration of creativity and collaboration, and new leadership from shared values. An extensive AI program was used in various stages. For example, a large conference was held with around 100 people. Not just employees, but also customers, suppliers, and people living in the direct vicinity of the factory. The conversations held with each other and the investigations produced fourteen new initiatives including one that resulted in their own training institute. Within two years, staff turnover dropped from 42% to 29% and the location was selected as one of the best workshops in Denver and Colorado.

After six years, considerable results were shown: increased productivity, better product quality, far fewer accidents in the workplace. Between 1995 and 2006, this achieved more than $ 25 million in cost savings and reduced waste. What do you see and hear when you now walk round the factory? People who regularly talk to each other about the state of things, what is going well, what is possible, and how you can build on this. The attention has shifted from problems to opportunities.

From the perspective of mindfulness, you can state what the power of the use of AI methods actually gives to organizations. What is most interesting in the study of AI is that organizations are better

---

22 David L. Cooperrider, Diana Whitney, and Jacquline M. Stavros, *Appreciative Inquiry Handbook* (San Franscisco: Baerrett-Koehler Publishers, 2008), 207-22. Masselink et al., *Waarderend organiseren.*

capable of dealing with everyday change and change in the environment.[23] It thus strengthens the resilience of organizations and that is the same as the resilience exercise from the previous chapter about mindful team work. What happens is that different competencies are strengthened. Firstly, the competence of directing attention at the strength and quality of the organization as the source of vitality. Then, the competence of being more visionary, looking more broadly, over the borders. Third, the competence to perform well, to give feedback from the feeling of making a genuine contribution. And finally, the competencies for collaborating are strengthened. What we see is that directing attention in the organization can also be of crucial importance.

In addition to seeing systems and appreciative inquiry, *scenario thinking* is a third way of recognizing patterns. An example that still inspires is Shell's approach at the start of the 1970s, even though we know that, in recent decades, Shell has passed through deep problems. At that time, Shell was confronted with the emergence of OPEC and new strengths and deviating patterns in the global oil market. The world was no longer stable and the old mental model no longer applied. Pierre Wack, then head of Shell's Group Planning, saw that things would have to be different because the future projections that his department produced did not lead to the change in insight in the managers concerned. Instead of announcing how it saw things, his department began to question the managers about assumptions for what, at that time, was a relatively stable future projection. And so, in the first months of 1973, they made use of a series of newly designed scenarios. Slowly the managers saw that the suppositions and the mental models on which these were based no longer reflected the complete truth and sometimes did not reflect the truth in any way. And, when in the winter of 1973-1974, OPEC announced an oil embargo, Shell reacted differently than other oil companies. The competition centralized management and reduced their divisions, but Shell did the opposite and gave its divisions more room to maneuver. They had

23 Cooperrider, Whitney, and Stavros, *Appreciative Inquiry Handbook*, 205-06.

realized that for a while turbulence would rule the industry and they adapted their organization to it. With spectacular results. In 1970, Shell was considered the "ugly sister" among the "seven sisters" (the name given to the seven major global oil companies at the time). Ten years later, people considered Shell the strongest, and, with Exxon, in a league above the others. Scenarios aimed at making mental models more flexible and improving them was a major part of that success.[24]

Drawing up scenarios[25]

Scenarios are internally consistent and challenging descriptions of possible futures. They deal with the circumstances in which you take decisions in the future. They deal with matters over which you essentially have no control, but which you can anticipate or arm yourself against. A scenario in this sense is something other than a summary of different choices you have to achieve your objective.

Scenarios such as these relate to the strategic conversation in the company or in the organization's network. They are stories that provide the context for discussions about strategy. Thus, scenarios are also stories that help the organizations or networks to experience learning processes and thus equip themselves for the future.

You draw up scenarios in a number of steps. Logically these begin with an orientation of the key problems and strategic issues. This is followed by an extensive investigation of the environment: which trends and developments are important for the future of the systems in which the organization or the network operates.

Based on this investigation, the most important uncertainties with the greatest impact on the future are then determined. And then the scenarios are constructed, using the key uncertainties.

We can then ask what we can learn based on these scenarios and

24 Senge, *De vijfde discipline*, 174-76.
25 Description derived from: Kees van der Heijden, *Scenario's. The Art of Strategic Conversation* (New York: John Wiley and Sons, 1996). And from: Jan Nekkers, *Wijzer in de toekomst. Werken met toekomstscenario's* (Amsterdam: Business Contact, 2007).

how the organization or network of stakeholders can take this into account as much as possible. Which strategies can be designed, which uncertainties reduced, which competences can be developed to handle this.

Shell still makes use of the scenario approach to direct the attention of the organization. Last year, an update of the scenarios for 2050, which Shell published in 2008, appeared which includes the most recent developments around the global financial and economic crisis. In the *Scramble* scenario, energy security of national governments is given priority over management of the demand for energy. Climate change drops down the list of priorities until disasters occur, major international tension about energy. In the other scenario, *Blueprints*, there is greater cohesion in policy between demand management, climate consequences, and the transition to new sources of energy. A new scenario for continuous slow economic development has been developed: *Depression 2.0*. A typical example of an organization that, using scenarios, is able to focus the attention of the organization on the environment in which it operates.[26]

The fourth field: innovation

The fourth field of attention that organizations have available in the context of mindfulness has to do with creativity, innovation, and rapidly learning new possibilities in the field of strategy development. All organizations must deal with a constantly changing environment: new generations of employees who make different demands, markets and customer demands that change, new policy measures by government, social issues that demand attention, such as diversity, climate, environment. The question is how you can direct the attention of the organization in such a way that you can anticipate all this.

It is therefore logical that you train the open mind that you have

26 Shell, *Signals & Signposts. Shell Energy Scenarios to 2050* (The Hague: Shell International, 2011). For more information see: www.shell.com/scenarios.

developed through mindfulness. A fine example of such an unexpected change in thinking is shown by the Belgian company Groep T. This training institute for engineers started advertising in 2008 in an attempt to recruit students. It used an interactive presentation which asked: how can an engineer help reduce the enormous use of air-conditioning in a Japanese office? The unexpected answer: by directing a campaign at Japanese businessmen to persuade them to adopt a different dress code. By getting them to change from a heavy wool suit into a short-sleeved shirt in the summer, a saving of more than 1.5 million tons of CO_2 could be achieved. Here, future engineers were challenged to think beyond the purely technical. It led to a question from Groep T to the Zen teacher, Edel Maex, of whether Buddhism could help train engineers in such a way that they become creative people instead of techno nerds. You can find his answer in the wonderful book *Open Mind*.[27]

An important way of developing innovative ideas is to travel and literally investigate foreign countries. Not just travelling from A to B, but to travel in such a way that you immerse yourself in an issue. An example. The Sustainable Food Lab is a consortium of companies, government, and non-profit organizations for the development of sustainable agriculture and the awareness that the agro-industry is facing crucial choices due to, on the one hand, a growing world population and, on the other, issues such as climate, water, biodiversity, and soil change. And yet nobody really expected that innovation in this field would happen just like that. In the words of André van Heemstra, former member of the management board of Unilever and one of the founders of the SFL: "creating models for sustainable agriculture demands bringing together parties who would not normally collaborate with each other. No matter how difficult that may be, there is really no other option because sustainably feeding nine billion people means changes that cannot be achieved by any one sector on its own."[28]

27 Edel Maex, *Open mind. Anders kijken naar de werkelijkheid* (Gent: Witsand Uitgevers, 2009).
28 Senge, *De noodzakelijke revolutie*, 44.

There is, therefore, a double challenge: creating both innovation and new forms of collaboration. For Hal Hamilton, director of the Lab, that was the first problem: how do I get a number of very busy, dedicated, and highly diverse people together, get them to address the situation and view a complicated and emotionally charged issue from their extremely different perspectives. With, on the one hand, the food producers who are accustomed to viewing technological solutions as the best way of increasing production. And on the other, the social organizations who combat the producers because they hold them responsible for the destruction of farming communities and ecological systems. And government is caught in the middle, because they must remain friends with both parties and must still find an answer to the pressure from companies to reduce prices and from organizations who support farmers who are being driven from their land. How on earth can you do that?

After an extensive initial stage, the breakthrough came during *learning journeys* to Brazil, which were undertaken by the whole group. The learning journeys to Brazil exposed both the strengths and the weaknesses of the food production systems. The journey was to major sugar and soya plantations, large processing installations for food and ethanol, cooperatives of small-scale farmers, coffee and sisal producers who tried to scrape together a living on small tracts of land, innovative specialized grape producers for the European market, and tracts of relatively unproductive land that were sold to landless workers. This was the first time that many of the activists had sat at the same table with people from the business community. And many of the latter acquired, for the first time, a new perspective on the situation of the small-scale country farmers. The group travelled together everywhere, so that there was a lot of time to exchange experiences and discuss different interpretations of the same situations. Initially, it all proved rather confusing, but ultimately the common experience broke through polite conversations or heated debates. Surprisingly, struggling with various experiences and images proved just as valuable as focusing on solving the world food problem: "it is not probable that we will do one without the other. We have got to know each other as people – not just as businessmen or citizens – and discover that there is no need to agree with each other all the time. And that's a good thing."[29]

A consequence of these learning journeys was the setting up of numerous innovative projects. These include: business models for sustainable trade relations, low carbon production systems, national food dialogues, and so on. The Sustainable Food Lab annually holds a new meeting in which learning journeys and new innovations are created.[30]

Learning journeys

In a learning journey, you bring together a diverse group of stakeholders who represent the system in which you are present as an organization and in which you wish to bring about change. They give the participants the possibility of learning about unknown and unusual environments, to immerse themselves in that situation and acquire relevant experiences. It is a journey that you take together.

The aim of a learning journey is to get the participants in a system working together on a series of activities such as experiencing, listening, studying, and dialogue. The objective is to create:

- A network of relationships between key stakeholders in that system.
- A shared understanding of the system's forces at work.
- Input for the development of innovative ideas that can lead to prototypes for far-reaching change.

The result is more acute attention for the various aspects of the system and for the various perspectives of the participants in the system. Just like new networks of relationships that contain the possibilities of mutual innovations.

A learning journey can take half a day or several days.

A second way of dealing with innovation and experimentation in an organization is to work regularly on making prototypes. David Kelley, the former CEO of IDEO, one of the world's most success-

29 Ibid., 246-48.
30 See the website: www.sustainablefoodlab.org.

ful design companies, calls this *thinking with your hands* which has a different quality than strict abstract thinking that is driven by planning and restricts itself to thought-up specifications.[31] The latter certainly has its value because working with prototypes is far more effective for creating new ideas and taking them on further. How does that use of prototypes work?

To start with, you must act against your intuition and accept an apparent loss of time by making sketches or models or building simulations. That building costs more time than thinking things up, doesn't it? What is, however, interesting is that we learn much faster by roughly building and testing than by completely building. The advantages of such a fast, rough, and cheap prototype is that you don't get particularly attached to it and you keep your eyes open for undesirable consequences and new options. And you achieve this with low costs. It is not about making a working model, but about getting a picture of the strengths and weaknesses of the idea and thus being able to improve it much quicker.[32]

Tim Brown, the current CEO of IDEO, describes the example of T-Mobile in Germany which – already many years ago – studied the possibilities of bringing together social groups via the telephone. And then it was not just about keeping in touch with each other but also sharing photos and messages, agendas, and all sorts of other things. In a way, that was much more direct than via the computer. The only way of actually doing this was to let a prototype of this service operate, for this was something you couldn't learn about if you did it on the drawing board. The design team set up two prototypes on a series of telephones (no, these weren't the smartphones we know today) and had two small groups of users get to work with them. Within two weeks it was clear which prototype worked the best. The winning idea gave people the possibility of building social networks around events in their lives. The other idea, people sharing their telephone books on their telephone, didn't prove a favorite.[33] Now

31 Tim Brown, *Change by Design* (New York: Harper Collins, 2009), 89.
32 Ibid., 90-91.
33 Ibid., 98.

we no longer think of that as surprising, considering the success of Facebook (which hardly existed when the experiment was held), but it was at the time.

You can also use making prototypes in the development of organizations and social systems. Brown gives the example of how they got IDEO through a life-threatening stage after the implosion of the dot-com bubble at the end of 2000. Scharmer describes how prototypes of new collaboration forms helped revitalize a regional health care system in Germany. Doctors and other professionals in health care showed little concern for the demands of insurers and governmental authorities, but instead entered into dialogues with patients and other stakeholders about the practical issues they encountered in their work. All questions and problems were discussed openly and groups arose which thought up practical solutions. Those prototypes were then quickly implemented and assessed. A consequence was that new ways were conceived with diabetic patients and then tried out for living healthily and becoming less dependent on medication. Other groups developed covenants for sharing expensive diagnostic equipment, exchanged doctors between hospitals, and improved collaboration for patients who had to deal with different institutions. This resulted in a new centre for emergencies with greater access for the patient: via the GP, the center itself, or via the specialized ambulance service. It is striking that patients in the region feel safer with this organization of care, the collaboration between doctors and paramedics has been improved, and in many places costs have been reduced. The process began with complicated and frustrating negotiations, but gained speed when doctors, paramedics, and patients started talking about their experiences, and it gained strength by developing prototypes that were then tested.[34]

---

34 Scharmer, *Theorie U. Leiding vanuit de toekomst die zich aandient,* 250-51.

Design-thinking and building prototypes[35]

Building prototypes has a number of important characteristics:

- It is based on and keeps in touch with inspiration sources: constantly open for new ideas.
- It is based on fast feedback: building a rough design (literally with your hands) in order to gain fresh ideas and make adjustments; improvising and seeing what happens.
- Leave the office and assess the prototypes with existing customers and stakeholders; show that it works.

In the process of developing prototypes, you can distinguish a number of steps:

1. Brainstorming and developing ideas.
2. Selection of ideas using the following criteria, in which you keep in touch with your original inspiration:
   a. Relevance
   b. Proper direction
   c. Revolutionary possibility
   d. Fast
   e. Rough design
   f. Leverage
   g. Repeatable and scalable
3. Build a rough model with your hands; learn from the building and the feedback.
4. Leave the office and see whether it works for customers and stakeholders.
5. If necessary, repeat the cycle several times.

"Fail fast to learn fast" is the motto of working with prototypes. At Cisco Systems, the technology company for network equipment and software, they call it Principle 0.8: no matter how large or com-

---

35 This description is based on: Brown, *Change by Design*, 106-07. And on the description of making prototypes on the website of the Presencing Institute: http://www.presencing.com/tools/prototyping (visited on 8 May 2012 at 12.02 pm). A fascinating video, "The Deep Dive," about the work of IDEO can be found on YouTube: http://www.youtube.com/watch?v=J kHOxyafGpE&feature=related (visited on 8 May 2012 at 12.14 pm).

prehensive your idea or project may be, you must present your first idea in a short time: not design 1.0 but design 0.8. You present something that is not yet finished, and thus provoke feedback that helps you forward![36]

The core of working with prototypes for organizations or networks is that you realize that change is inevitable and that everything is, even if it appears to be solid and strong, a prototype. A prototype is never something that is immaculate – no, it is always in a shape that can teach us something; about our objectives, our process, and ourselves.[37] When we make prototypes we swing between *mindless action* and an *actionless mind*[38], between just doing something without insight and doing absolutely nothing because the situation is so overwhelming. Mindfulness makes organizations resilient toward accepting the discomfort associated with an unfinished situation, while at the same time it maintains a critical awareness and openness for change.

The ways of working mentioned above come together in charting a new course in the value creation of an organization. In order to find a new direction, the organization takes conscious steps to pause, to recognize, and to investigate what there is, and to let go of existing mental models in order to look at what the situation (market, society) asks of it.

The U-process as social technology for change

Strategy development with full attention can be very well addressed using the U-process designed by Scharmer. You could view this as a social technology for change based on mindfulness or awareness. For a complete description of this, I would refer you to his book and here will limit myself to the core model of this process.[39]

36 Scharmer, *Theorie U. Leiding vanuit de toekomst die zich aandient*, 256.
37 Brown, *Change by Design*, 105.
38 Scharmer, *Theorie U. Leiding vanuit de toekomst die zich aandient*, 252.
39 Ibid.

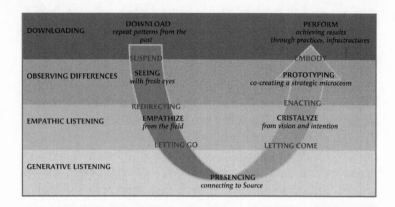

This approach was put into practice during the strategy formation process of Triodos Bank in the Netherlands in 2008 and 2009. Triodos is a pioneer in the field of sustainable banking, but at the end of 2007 the bank grew less than the total market for sustainable banking. Had the bank become redundant? Today, Triodos is once again exhibiting striking growth, thanks to the new strategy, in which opinion leadership and practical products form the core for customers. Striking elements in this expedition toward value, which is comparable in many ways to Scharmer's U-process, are: customer safaris (learning journeys), extended stages of acknowledging and investigating issues, making use of prototypes and design thinking ("fail fast to learn fast"), and the great influence of mindful, that is, conscious leadership. The director plays a crucial role at important moments of transition from word to deed by embodying where the attention of the organization must be directed.[40] The power of mindfulness in such an approach is that you effectively involve both the cognitive and emotional sides, and the importance of this has been long established in organizational science. Fundamental and broadly supported change can only arise if there is intensive learning and engagement at an individual level, so that the autopilot and the immunity to change are breached.

40 Paul Kloosterboer and Hein Dijksterhuis, "De strategische ontdekkingstocht van Triodos Bank Nederland," *Holland Management Review*, no. 138 (2011). And also: Paul Kloosterboer, *Expeditie naar waarde. Strategie ontdekken met professionals* (Den Haag: Academic Service, 2011).

Embedding mindfulness in the organization

The transition process toward an organization that can flexibly switch from the autopilot where routine rules to full attention to direct itself to the future is not a linear or an easy transition. To start with, such a change must have a reason and sometimes more than one. In many cases, the reasons for change come from outside the organization or they arise because a group of organizations or a network gains the insight that their contribution to production or service provision must take a new tack and go farther than the boundaries of their own organization. Often, when change is announced, reference is made to the external threat or reason. But for real change, this is not always handy and in any case people will not change faster because of it.

Every change is always, in a psychological sense, the negation of what has always applied until then and thus inevitably causes turmoil and anxiety.[41] It is therefore not without reason that the presence of a realistic aspiration is necessary, as we saw in the previous chapter, but is not sufficient on its own. Greater attention must be paid to developing psychological safety in which change can take place, and this makes the presence of a green zone of mindfulness of crucial importance.

Many factors must be addressed when creating such psychological safety: a positive vision, involvement in one's own learning trajectory, good possibilities for training and education, learning by doing, role models and support groups. And these factors must all be in order together.[42]

Essentially, it is a process in which the people who form the organization or the network under change together have the courage to tell each other "what happens and is happening here" and what could or should happen. Creating mutual significance[43] or cognitive redefinition[44] and culture change – for that is what it is

41 Schein, *De bedrijfscultuur als ziel van de onderneming*, 105.
42 Ibid., 110.
43 Froukje D. Wirtz, "Management van het onverwachte" (bookreview), *M&O* 66, no. 1 (2012): 90.
44 Schein, *De bedrijfscultuur als ziel van de onderneming*, 111-12.

– touches the very being or soul of an organization.

An organizational culture has developed in response to internal and external challenges for which a solution must be found. That applies equally to organizations that have just been set up and are strongly entrepreneurial and to organizations that have passed through various life cycles and have built up a more rigid culture. Cultural change is ultimately about adjusting people's behavior that emerges as an answer that is considered valid in the situation. And for that, the challenge or problem must be clearly experienced and addressed before any sensible change can take place. One study shows that most cultural programs that concentrate purely on behavioral change are not effective. These only become effective if there is cohesion between a newly written description of the significance of the organization and a change of vision, strategy, structure, and work processes.[45]

One thing is certain: if you want to change everything at once in the direction of mindfulness, you will almost certainly fail. So start with small steps, but steps based on a clear approach and vision. Also accept that people will initially put the new mindfulness culture into practice as an espoused theory, an expressed value that you will find in some actions and that it will only become a genuine productive theory-in-use (model II) in the course of time, before ultimately becoming a fixed component of the culture.[46] Do not implement any culture program directed at mindfulness, but make the mindfulness practices and attitudes explained here part of the intervention for increasing productivity and motivation, so that customers and stakeholders can be supplied with greater value. Education and training in the instruments of mindfulness can play an important role in this and they will then acquire a natural importance for the employees and the organization.

Every change starts with pausing and designing an approach for effectuating change. Because culture isn't something you create just like that, the process requires endurance, and will take months

45 Boonstra, *Leiders in cultuurverandering*, 40.
46 Argyris, *Organizational Traps*, 64.

or even years. And the process must be nourished and supported all that time. Sometimes this can be through symbolic actions. If you wish to create mindfulness, you could perhaps introduce a standard time for peace and quiet, for example at the start of meetings. Or to demonstrate explicitly as manager or leader that you take short meditative breathing pauses. It helps to set an example. Or you take the practices of mindful organizing discussed in this chapter as a starting point for various activities in the organization. It is about defining new norms and rules with each other and holding each other to them. You can do this playfully but sometimes seriously, and particularly using your mindful leadership.

Leadership in strategy and cultural change means helping the organization or the network breach borders that they immediately encounter with fundamental change and innovation: the voices of habit ("we always do it like that"), of cynicism ("don't think that'll work") and of fear of change ("do I really want to change?").[47]

Initiatives and leadership in cultural change can be supported by many and do not need to come only from the top. It is increasingly a social process of giving and taking in shared leadership.[48] But leadership remains crucial in achieving a change of course. We saw that in the example of strategy development at Triodos. Mindful leadership sets the tone and acts as an anchor for the norms that are important in an organization.

---

47 Scharmer, *Theorie U. Leiding vanuit de toekomst die zich aandient*, 294-95.
48 See the presentation by: Erik van der Loo, "Psychogische kijk op het nieuwe werken," in *Het nieuwe werken* (Utrecht: Veldhoen + Company, 2010).

References

Argyris, Chris. *Organizational Traps*. Oxford: Oxford University Press, 2010.

Boonstra, Jaap. *Leiders in cultuurverandering*. Stichting Management Studies. Assen: Van Gorcum, 2011.

Brown, Tim. *Change by Design*. New York: Harper Collins, 2009.

Bryan, Bill, Michael Goodman, and Jaap Schaveling. *Systeemdenken. Ontdekken van onze organisatiepatronen*. Den Haag: Academic Service, 2006.

Cooperrider, David L., Diana Whitney, and Jacquline M. Stavros. *Appreciative Inquiry Handbook*. San Franscisco: Baerrett-Koehler Publishers, 2008.

Dalen, Bert van, Bert Slagmolen, and Robert Taen. *Mindful organiseren*. Apollo 13 Consult, 2009.

Dijkstra, Jelle, and Paul-Peter Feld. *Gedeeld leiderschap: veerkacht door nieuwe vormen van samenwerken, organiseren, leren en leiderschap*. 2012.

Goleman, Daniel, Richard Boyatzis, and Annie McKee. *Primal Leadership. Realizing the Power of Emotional Intelligence*. Boston: Harvard Business School Press, 2002.

Heijden, Kees van der. *Scenario's. The Art of Strategic Conversation*. New York: John Wiley and Sons, 1996.

Kloosterboer, Paul. *Expeditie naar waarde. Strategie ontdekken met professionals*. Den Haag: Academic Service, 2011.

———. "Navigeren bij strategievorming, lessen uit de literatuur." *M&O*, no. 5 (2008).

Kloosterboer, Paul, and Hein Dijksterhuis. "De strategische ontdekkingstocht van Triodos Bank Nederland." *Holland Management Review*, no. 138 (2011): 8-17.

Langer, Ellen. *The Power of Mindful Learning*. Cambridge: Perseus Books, 1997.

Loo, Erik van der. "Psychogische kijk op het nieuwe werken." In *Het nieuwe werken*. Utrecht: Veldhoen + Company, 2010.

Maex, Edel. *Open mind. Anders kijken naar de werkelijkheid*. Gent: Witsand Uitgevers, 2009.

Masselink, Robert, Rombout van den Nieuwenhof, Joep. C. de Jong, and Annemarie van Iren. *Waarderend organiseren*. Amsterdam: Gelling Publicaties, 2008.

Meadows, Donella H. *Thinking in Systems. A Primer.* London: Earthscan, 2008.

Nekkers, Jan. *Wijzer in de toekomst. Werken met toekomstscenario's.* Amsterdam: Business Contact, 2007.

Noonan, William R. *Discussing the Undiscussable. A Guide to Overcoming Defensive Routines in the Workplace.* San Francisco: Jossey-Bass, 2007.

Rosenberg, Marshall B. *Geweldloze communicatie.* Rotterdam: Lemniscaat, 2007.

Scharmer, C. Otto. *Theorie U. Leiding vanuit de toekomst die zich aandient.* Zeist: Christofoor, 2010.

Schein, Edgar H. *De bedrijfscultuur als ziel van de onderneming.* Schiedam: Scriptum, 2008.

Senge, Peter. *De noodzakelijke revolutie.* Den Haag: Academic Service, 2009.

———. *De vijfde discipline.* Schiedam: Scriptum, 1992.

Senge, Peter, Art Kleiner, Charlotte Roberts, Richard Ross, George Roth, and Bryan Smith. *De vijfde discipline. Praktijkboek.* Den Haag: Academic Service, 2006.

Shell. *Signals & Signposts. Shell Energy Scenarios to 2050.* The Hague: Shell International, 2011.

Weick, Karl E., and Kathleen M. Sutcliffe. *Managing the Unexpected.* San Francisco: John Wiley & Sons, 2010.

Wirtz, Froukje D. "Management van het onverwachte (boekbespreking)." *M&O* 66, no. 1 (Januari/Februari 2012, 2012): 88-95.

Epilogue
Mastering mindful leadership

*"Just as a farmer irrigates his fields, just as a fletcher fashions
an arrow, just as a carpenter sheds a block of wood, so does the
sage tame the self."*[1]

Buddha – *Dhammapada*

Mastery of the conscious response

At the start of this book, I wrote that teams and organizations are
constantly changing. High performance is expected, more intensive teamwork and profound innovation, not only to serve customers better but also to address important economic and social
issues.

Management guru Peter Drucker stated that it was crucial for
the survival of organizations that they systematically let go of old
and no longer useful ways of working in order to create space for
innovation.[2] And the urgency has only increased. But change
does not take place so easily, because we must first gain insight into our autopilot of routine action, and once we start changing we
have to face our inclination to make ourselves immune to change
because it generates too much fear and uncertainty. That is true on
a personal level, but also in our organizations. What's more, as a

1 Stephen Batchelor, *Confessions of a Buddhist Atheist* (New York: Spiegel
and Grau, 2010). 152.
2 Jeremy Hunter, "Knowledge Worker Productivity and the Practice of Self-
Management," in *The Drucker Difference*, ed. Graig L. Pearce, Joseph A.
Maciarello, and Hideki Yamawaki (New York: McGraw Hill, 2010). 186.

society we are faced with issues concerning food for a growing world population, climate, water, and energy, and we still have no solutions for these. Challenges indeed.

In this book I have shown you how you can develop the five dimensions of mindful leadership in order to address all these challenges. By increasing your ability for mindfulness, you strengthen:

- Resilience
- Fearless presence of mind
- Taking unconditional responsibility
- Investigative openness
- Experimental, innovative, and connecting action.

With mindfulness, you learn to switch between action and reflection, between doing and being. You replace the autopilot with the mastery of the conscious response. As a mindful leader you create a green zone of mindfulness, not only for yourself but also in your team and you establish space for learning. And, in the same way, you also take the next step: directing, as an organization, your full attention on matters that you are doing in the outside world: delivering products and services to customers, taking into account the demands of the social environment.

Through the mastery of the mindful response, you create room for making a contribution to solving the major issues facing organizations or networks. Improving what already exists is no longer sufficient; solutions must be sought that are not obvious, and are in unknown territory. For it is necessary that organizations and networks – and the individuals within them – open themselves for observation, the awareness, and the choices that are asked of them: mindful from the perspective of the future. Otto Scharmer, one of the founders of this approach, calls this *presencing*. It is not just about improving the organizational system, but rather about regeneration, the renewal of its very foundations.[3] You renew the

3 C. Otto Scharmer, *Theorie U. Leiding vanuit de toekomst die zich aandient* (Zeist: Christofoor, 2010). 63 and 84.

connection between the aspiration of the organization and everybody's individual contribution, but on a higher level, namely what
the environment or customers and other stakeholders need from
us.

Mindful leadership: character and connectedness

By practicing mindfulness in your leadership, your skills increase
because mindfulness is by nature and origin a practical approach.
Anybody who goes back to the stories of Siddharta Gotama, the
Buddha, sees that for him it was not about losing self or emptying
self, it was, for Gotama, all about creating character and will-pow-
er.

The core is practice, developing a practice of skill: "Just as a
farmer irrigates his fields, just as a fletcher fashions an arrow, just as
a carpenter sheds a block of wood, so does the sage tame the self,"
says the Buddha.[4] Self is a field that is ploughed, an arrow that is
fashioned, a block of wood that is shaped. The development of the
self arises in the action.

Whoever follows this path of craftsmanship will notice that his or
her relationship with the world changes. To start with, you will
notice that mindful action combats old patterns. You discover
that, with the better antenna of body and mind, you develop a
sharper eye for the struggle, the fear and the disharmony in daily
life. Something which you cannot only observe with the mind.

You simply cannot avoid asking yourself whether you are acting
with integrity. Anybody who acts from mindfulness notices that
their actions are not purely and exclusively directed at a goal, but realize that it is part of a larger whole and not just of themselves. In this
way, it is fundamentally different from ego-centric action.[5]

Mindful action has wider implications. It is not only aimed at developing your own character but also connects itself with the fu-

---

4 Batchelor, *Confessions of a Buddhist Atheist*: 151.
5 Rodney Smith, *Stepping out of Self-Deception* (Boston: Shambhala, 2010).
  127.

ture of the surrounding world. With mindfulness you cannot do, even as an organization, anything other than stand in the very center of life. Mindfulness shares this with its Buddhist source of inspiration. For although the latter has a long history of monasteries and meditation in seclusion, the essence is all about learning to deal with all facets of everyday life.

Organizations that set to work mindfully, notice that their teams function well and are better able to address the constantly changing demands of customers and other stakeholders. And they don't walk away from the responsibility – in a world that is globalized and burdened with various crises (around food, energy, climate, religion, and culture, to name just a few) – to make life on this earth sustainable: for the possibility that people and other life on earth shall flourish for the length of days.[6] They bring the fearless presence of mind to accept this and take the unconditional responsibility to work on the profound innovation required for it.

The practice of mindfulness with its two sides of the coin, the development of attentiveness and the associated attitude – the flame and the heat together – invites everybody, time and time again, to compassion, to efforts for the good, to contribution to the well-being of the other. In short, to a moral and distinctive involvement with the future of mankind and our planet.

6 My understanding of flourishing is inspired by the beautiful notion of sustainability as "the possibility that humans and other life will *flourish* on the Earth *forever*" by John Ehrenfeld. See John Ehrenfeld, *Sustainability by Design* (New Haven and London: Yale University Press, 2008).

References

Batchelor, Stephen. *Confessions of a Buddhist Atheist.* New York: Spiegel and Grau, 2010.

Ehrenfeld, John. *Sustainability by Design.* New Haven and London: Yale University Press, 2008.

Hunter, Jeremy. "Knowledge Worker Productivity and the Practice of Self-Management." Chap. 11 In *The Drucker Difference*, edited by Graig L. Pearce, Joseph A. Maciarello, and Hideki Yamawaki. 175-94. New York: McGraw Hill, 2010.

Scharmer, C. Otto. *Theorie U. Leiding vanuit de toekomst die zich aandient.* Zeist: Christofoor, 2010.

Smith, Rodney. *Stepping out of Self-Deception.* Boston: Shambhala, 2010.

Acknowledgements

This book has a history and I would like to thank a number of people who have inspired and/or helped me.

When I participated in mindfulness training in the spring of 2007, I remarked at the end that I wondered how I could use mindfulness in my work as a management consultant. Several weeks later, Rob Brandsma, the trainer, invited me to think about this with him. Rob and I have subsequently studied the subject of mindfulness and leadership together, developed training programs for managers, and ultimately incorporated all this in the Center for Mindfulness, which we set up together with George Langenberg. The first idea for this book arose in a discussion we had together. Rob has since become a valuable colleague and dear friend, and I am thankful for his initiative.

Jon Kabat-Zinn had the brilliant, genial idea to incorporate mindfulness into a Western training format and thus make mindfulness available outside Buddhism. He laid the foundation for an effective approach to stress and pain and inspired others to employ mindfulness in other areas of life, such as leadership in organizations.

I would like to thank my Dutch mindfulness teachers Johan Tinge and Frits Koster for their practical and wise instruction. The mindfulness meditation retreats with Frits have each time been a welcome deepening of insight and connection.

In addition to mindfulness, other important sources of inspiration for this book include the work of Ed Schein about cultural change in organizations, that of Peter Senge about learning organizations and that of Otto Scharmer about Theory U, a social technology for change processes, all at the Massachusetts Institute of

Technology. Peter and Otto know like no others how to connect the complex changes in society and the way you consciously deal with your reactions to them. Together with the team of the Presencing Institute: Arawana Hayashi, Beth Jandernoa, Katrin Käufer, Kelvy Bird, and others, they provide a living example of mindful leadership.

In recent years, I have learned much from the people with whom I have worked in various roles. I may perhaps forget a few, but I would certainly like to mention: Felix Cohen, Joost Drenthe, Frits Hermans, Klaske de Jonge, Leen van Leersum, Marike van Lier Lels, and Jan Bouke Wijbrandi. Naturally, also my teams at the Consumentenbond, Oxfam Novib, Emergis, and the Nature & Environment Foundation. Also my colleagues in the training program to become a mindfulness teacher. And the participants in my MBSR and Mindfulness for Managers programs, who had the courage to discuss openly their experiences and thus gave me the chance to deepen my insight into the possibilities of mindful leadership.

My colleagues in the Masterclass 2010-2012 of the Presencing Institute. I cannot thank all 80 of them here, but I can make an exception for my peer group: Julie Arts, Marian Goodman, Theo Konijn, Kasee Mhoney, and Megan Seneque. Thank you for your support, inspiration, and trust in this project.

Nor have I done all the writing for the book on my own. Dick Benschop drew my attention to an inspiring book about *"conscious business"* some time ago. Thanks also to the people who sometimes read extracts and considered it perfectly normal that this book would be published: Alexander Schwedeler, Susan Skej, Martin Büchele, Ursula Versteegen, Gene Toland, Jim Marsden, Phil Cass, Gregor Barnum, Beth Jandernoa, and Arawana Hayashi. The same is true for Hein Dijksterhuis, who showed instant enthusiasm about the subject during our flights to meetings of the PI masterclass. As did Willem van Spijker, Jurry Swart, Paul Engel, and Marc Hijkoop. My colleagues at Reos Partners – Zaid Hassan, Mille Bojer, and Mia Eisenstadt – gave me the opportunity to try out mindfulness practices in international change processes. I worked on this with Hendrik Tiesinga and Leonie Stekelenburg in the Netherlands, and with Christine Wank in Germany. Arjen Oosterbaan provided excellent video work on our mindfulness trainings. And in recent months, Ruud Schuurs and Marleen Janssen Groesbeek often took over jobs for me for our Pure Winst platform.

Rob Brandsma, Ernst Harting, Teun Oosterbaan, and Erik Heydelberg were my readers as I wrote. Their insight, enthusiasm, and critical comments helped me enormously. I would also like to thank my Dutch publisher, Annemie Michels, for her faith in the book right from the first idea. Also thanks to my editor, Pim van Tol, for his crucial input and for his belief that a translation into English would become a reality; he also brought structure and clarity to the book. I thank Wardy Poelstra for his project management in the production of this English version.

A special thanks to my American friends and colleagues, especially to Chris Germer, who not only showed me what it means to embody a compassionate attitude but also supported me to publish this translation at crucial point in time.

My family and friends who gave me their intense support. And finally thanks to my wife Marie-Claire, who played such an important role in the creation of this book. She thought along with me and inspired me, was my highly critical reader, and suggested countless important literature references. And in addition she created the space in which I could work on this book without distraction. I thank you for your wonderful love!

About the author

Wibo Koole is both a management consultant and leadership expert, operating from his own business, Create2connect. And one of the founders and directors of the Center for Mindfulness in Amsterdam, where he teaches mindfulness programs for managers and for corporations. His work focuses on strategy and innovation, change management, and leadership development in a wide range of organizations, both corporate and social.

He also has considerable experience in management, as campaign and strategy manager with the Dutch Consumers' Association, as head of communications for Oxfam Novib, and the mental health organization, Emergis, and as general director of the Dutch Nature and Environment Foundation. He has inside knowledge of many economic sectors: telecommunications and internet technology, agro-production, health care, and banking and insurance; he has also worked with the government. He was also politically active as chairman of the PvdA (Dutch Labor Party) in Amsterdam.

In addition, he has held the position of administrator and supervisory director at various foundations and was Chairman of the Supervisory Board of the AMC/De Meren, a major psychiatric center in Amsterdam. Until 2012, he was member of the Advisory Board of the insurance company Delta Lloyd and is now member of the Customer Council of the General Pension Group (APG), the executive body of the General Citizens Pension Fund (ABP). Recently he founded a platform that focuses on creating a sustainable financial sector.

He has been a mindfulness teacher since 2008. He regularly gives the Mindfulness Based Stress Reduction basic program with open enrolment. In addition, he developed one of the first mindfulness training programs for leaders (in 2009), in collaboration with his colleague and mindfulness trainer, Rob Brandsma. Within the Center for Mindfulness, he leads the mindfulness, management and leadership program.

Wibo Koole graduated with honors in political science from the University of Amsterdam, and took the Advanced Management Program at the Wharton Business School (University of Pennsylvania, Philadelphia, USA). He is also a certified transformational coach. As a management consultant he is closely connected to the Presencing Institute at MIT (Boston), that initiates and facilitates collective mindful leadership for complex transformation processes in organizations and society.

He can be reached at:
www.centrumvoormindfulness.nl
www.create2connect.nl

List of exercises

Index

12421037R00125

Printed in Great Britain
by Amazon.co.uk, Ltd.,
Marston Gate.